NO PLACE
FOR A LADY

NO PLACE FOR A LADY

Tales of Adventurous Women Travelers

Barbara Hodgson

Ten Speed Press
Berkeley, California

ENDPAPERS: *"A Visit to the Harem in Morocco" (detail). R. Caton Woodville,* ILN, *17 December 1887: 727.*

HALF-TITLE PAGE: *Adapted from* Our Journey Around the World with Glimpses of Life in Far Off Lands as Seen Through a Woman's Eyes *by Rev. Francis E. Clark and Harriet E. Clark, Hartford, Conn.: A.D. Worthington, 1894.*

FRONTISPIECE: *"A Lady Mountaineer, Mountaineering in the Tyrol: Turning a Corner." R. Caton Woodville,* ILN, *18 September 1886: 298.*

PAGES vi–vii: *A woman and her guide in front of the Sphinx. Postcard, c. 1900.*

Credits for chapter opening images can be found on page 212.

Ten Speed Press
Box 7123
Berkeley, California 94707
www.tenspeed.com

Originally published in Canada by Greystone Books.

Library of Congress Cataloging-in-Publication Data on file with the publisher.

Edited by Nancy Flight
Design by Barbara Hodgson/Byzantium Books

All uncredited images are from Byzantium Archives. Images without attribution are from unknown sources or by unknown artists. Every effort has been made to trace accurate ownership of copyrighted text and visual material used in this book. Errors or omissions will be corrected in subsequent editions, provided notification is sent to the publisher.

Printed and bound in Hong Kong by C & C Offset Printing Co., Ltd.

1 2 3 4 5 6 7 8 9 10 — 06 05 04 03 02

Contents

LADY HESTER STANHOPE.

London Henry Colburn 1845.

Introduction
Everywhere but Home

THE RUMBLE OF HOOVES echoed across the desert long before the horses and their riders materialized, heightening an already palpable excitement. Rumours had been circulating in Palmyra for days that a caravan would be coming from Damascus, bringing a most unusual visitor. As the Palmyrans turned their darkly tanned faces towards the hills to the west, a cry rang out; someone had spotted distant figures. Responding as though to a signal, hundreds of men leapt onto their horses and, brandishing swords, raced through the ruins of Zenobia's fabled city to meet the new arrivals. The remaining townspeople—men, women and children—waited impatiently as the party descended into their valley. At last they could see a tall, imposing woman in the lead, dressed in a fine woollen robe, astride a handsome white stallion. As the entourage passed, the crowd cheered the imperious foreigner, Lady Hester Stanhope, the self-proclaimed Queen of the Desert.

The year was 1819, and Stanhope had just done the unthinkable. She had travelled, independently and unveiled, to the heart of Syria, where no European woman and few European men had openly visited since Roman times. In doing so, she abandoned her constrained life and landed in the thick of adventure, behaviour not normally associated with women of days gone by. And she wasn't the only one to defy propriety through travel; there were countless others.

Many of us believe that women in the past were shackled by lack of income or by wifely, motherly or daughterly duties. We think that biased attitudes towards women's abilities must have curtailed freedom and encouraged physical and emotional dependence on menfolk. That these constraints existed there can be no doubt, yet there is a vast library of travel literature written by women who seemed to be oblivious to them. It's true that money was a problem, as it is now, but many women did have incomes, sometimes from inheritances, but often

Hester Stanhope. The likeness is suspect, as no known portraits were done of Stanhope in her lifetime. Attributed to R. J. Hamerton, Meryon, vol. 1, frontispiece.

from work, including travel writing. Family duties did tie them down—it's one reason so many waited until middle age to travel—but as soon as they could cut free, they did. Attitudes were restrictive, but not to the degree we assume. Dependence was encouraged, but all the same, many women did as they wished. Women were anything but helpless, though they could be maddeningly so if it suited them. And women, more than men, had to justify their travels, so an astonishing number searched for intellectual stimulation. This yearn to learn got them collecting or researching.

Seventeenth- to nineteenth-century women travellers could be roughly divided into two categories: middle-class women whose home lives were monotonous, and upper-class women whose wealth led to a steady diet of instability. For the former, travel was a way of breaking the tedium and lassitude; it's fascinating to read of their acceptance of such inconveniences as fleas, as if the irritation of the bug bites reminded them that they were finally very much alive. For the latter, restlessness became a habit that had to be maintained at all costs.

Marianne North.
After a photo by Williams, Dronsart, 385.

The women in these categories travelled for any of a number of specific reasons. Some had no choice; they were banished from their native country. Caroline of Brunswick, whose dislike of her husband, the Prince of Wales, was returned in spades, was exiled because of bad behaviour; outspoken Mme de Staël fled France during the revolution, then was exiled by Napoleon; Jane Digby, Lady Ellenborough, took a Continental "holiday" to have a baby that was not her husband's. Little did she know that this moral slip would lead her to great adventure in Syria. In 1739, complaining that "there is no part of the world where our sex is treated with so much contempt [as in England]," Lady Mary Wortley Montagu went to the Continent, and then to Italy, where she remained until 1761.[1] Her comment may have been a handy smokescreen to hide her pursuit of a potential lover.

Some women, including painter Marianne North, roamed to get over the death of a loved one. Others travelled as part of their wifely duties; Eliza Fay, writing of her India adventure, declared, "I undertook the journey with a view of preserving my husband from destruction, for had I not accompanied him . . . he would never, never, I am convinced, have reached Bengal."[2]

Religion provided another excuse. Many women, including the above-mentioned Princess Caroline, dared the hazardous pilgrimage to Jerusalem; and others—Mrs. G. Albert Rogers, author of *A Winter in Algeria* (1865), for one—audaciously handed out religious tracts while vacationing.

Invalidism, in part, drove the indomitable Isabella Bird around the world; Lucie Duff Gordon migrated to Egypt every winter, and eventually settled there, on account of tuberculosis. Similarly, there was a desperate and universal desire to escape the damp, cold north for the warmly scented south.

But the best reason to travel may have been for no reason at all. Ida Pfeiffer spent her girlhood dreaming of the open road. Mary Shelley viewed travel as an all-encompassing passion that was incomprehensible to those who weren't similarly driven.

British women, more than any other group, abandoned themselves to this passion, resulting in a disproportionate number of British women in these pages. The *Quarterly Review* declared that other nations "have not the same well-read, solid thinking,—early rising—sketch-loving—light-footed—trim-waisted—straw-hatted specimen of women; educated with the refinement of the highest classes, and with the usefulness of the lowest."★[3]

This doesn't mean that women on the Continent did not travel; they did and in large numbers, for Europeans, like the British, circled the globe in the name of adventure and colonialism.

Although less is known about women of non-European backgrounds, we can see from comments by European travellers that a desire to travel was not universal. Scottish-born Frances Calderón de la Barca observed that Mexican women in Europe felt as though they were exiled from their homeland and couldn't wait to return. Harriet Martineau was told that in Egypt European women were pitied because they travelled, but in Asyut, Lucie Duff Gordon saw a young Egyptian woman who chose both to dress as a man and to travel; her predilections were accepted by other Egyptians. Flora Tristan, a French traveller to Peru in the 1830s, wrote that the women she met in the town of Arequipa "seize eagerly upon any occasion for travel . . . and no amount of

---

★ This description was a touch fanciful; some British travellers, like Fanny Trollope, though thoroughly knowledgeable, were rotund rather than trim, and walked not with a light foot but with "colossean strides unattainable by any but English women."[4]

expense or fatigue can deter them."[5] Just how true this was, we'll see later when we meet Peruvian Isabella Godin des Odonais.

North American women, too, got about. Isabella Bird called herself "a limp, ragged, shoeless wretch" compared with her temporary companion on the Sandwich Islands, Miss Karpe, a "typical American travelling lady, who is encountered everywhere from the Andes to the Pyramids, tireless, with indomitable energy, Spartan endurance, and a genius for attaining everything."[6]

What did spur British women to travel more than their counterparts elsewhere? Both British men and women were zealous wanderers and colonizers (as is evident from the huge swaths of pink on nineteenth-century world maps). Marie Dronsart, writing in 1894, attributed British women's mania for travel to the spirit of adventure that seemed to possess all British.[7] But possibly the greatest encouragement they had came from reading travel literature. No other country produced as many books on the subject; through this means women travellers were able to tear down the barriers that had until then held them back.

Understanding the role of women's travel writing is pivotal to our understanding of seventeenth- to nineteenth-century women travellers. Not only are their adventures revealed, so are their attitudes towards the opposite sex, other women and other cultures. Women travel writers also give us views of political events, the mechanics of travel and society in other lands, filling in gaps left by male observers. And through their writing, they influenced thousands of readers and contributed to the growth of travel.

Women wrote about their travels for a variety of reasons: to justify their leisure time by converting it into labour, to entertain those cooped up back home, to finance future journeys or to express their sincere interest in recording all they saw. A woman travel writer may have been a rare thing in the eighteenth century, but by 1817, as Eliza Fay wrote, they were so common they were no longer "object[s] of derision."[8] By 1845, some were considered professionals; the *Quarterly Review* declined to review works by women who would systematically "make a tour in order to make a book." The amateurs praised by the *Quarterly Review* benefited, so the magazine claimed, "from the very *purposelessness* resulting from the more desultory nature of [their] education."[9] Still, it wasn't something that everyone wished to put her name on, so

dozens of books appeared anonymously, under the rubrics of "A Lady," as in Mrs. Vigor's *Letters from a Lady, Who Resided Some Years in Russia* (1775), or "A Resident," as the author of *The Englishwoman in India* (1864) called herself.

Perhaps European women considered their activities too insignificant to write about, or fewer publishers were willing to take on their work. Exceptions include Jane Dieulafoy from France, Isabelle Eberhardt from Switzerland, Johanna Schopenhauer from Germany, Ida Pfeiffer from Austria, Lydie Paschkoff from Russia and Cristina di Belgiojoso from Italy. To make matters worse, relatively little that does exist has been translated. The non-English books that did reach English readers left the *Quarterly Review* unimpressed. That periodical complained that French women travellers couldn't spell and that German women saw things inwardly not outwardly, hence their inability for "rapid observation."[10]

Ida Pfeiffer is an example of how the *Quarterly Review* had wrongly perceived German-speaking

A ship's employee diplomatically collects tickets from the ladies of a harem on a Turkish steamer.

G. Dorand, engraving by Roberts, *Graphic*, 24 March 1877: 269.

⬎"We have had *The Englishwoman in Russia, The Englishwoman in Thibet, The Englishwoman in America,* and the Englishwoman in almost every hole and corner of the globe. If our beautiful countrywomen carry out this mania for travelling much further, the greatest novelty our publishers could give us will be,—*The Englishwoman in England."— Punch*[11]

VÉRITABLE EXTRAIT DE VIANDE LIEBIG

VÉRITABLE EXTRAIT DE VIANDE LIEBIG

Cards published by Liebig's Meat Extract, c. 1880, showed women getting to the fashionable corners of the world; Athens, Yalta, Algeria and Cairo were just four examples. The cards were designed to encourage travellers to take Liebig's with them wherever they went.

Annie Brassey bartering with Fuegians. No one seems concerned that the traders haven't got a stitch of clothing on.
Brassey 1878, 22.

women travel writers. The succinct comments that fill her books, which were translated into English and French, display a well-honed talent for turning observation into riveting narratives. Although Pfeiffer denounced those who exaggerated their mishaps just to make a juicy story, her unadorned accounts of an attempt on her life in the Brazilian jungle and of Borneo headhunters increased her popularity with fans of travel literature.

Then, as now, the more exciting the trip, the better the sales of the book. But if thrills were lacking, sarcasm would do. English traveller Frances Elliot wrote several scathing books as part of her *Idle Woman* series. Spain, Italy and Constantinople, targets of her scornful pen, never looked so bad or sold so well. Lazy servants, dishonest innkeepers, vermin, dust storms and intoxicated boors were all featured.

But bugs and drunkards were safe subjects. Unfortunately, most women refrained from including details that might cast themselves in a bad light. Because their books usually took the form of a diary or letters and were written or edited after the fact, it was simple to purposely omit details about hygiene, for instance, or worse, diarrhoea. Lady Montagu scandalized her readers by discussing the intimacies of the Turkish harem and even referred to her own corsets. Almost 150 years after Montagu's *Letters* (1725) first appeared, Lady Charlotte Bury wrote that one never admitted reading them, "for they are deemed so naughty by all the world, that one must keep up one's reputation for modesty, and try to blush whenever they are mentioned." Fanny Parks, in contrast, confessed that Montagu's works "rendered her very anxious" to visit a zenana, the Indian harem.[12]

～"The only use of a gentleman in traveling is to look after the luggage, and we take care to have no luggage."—[Emily Lowe], *Unprotected Females in Norway*[14]

Speaking of unspeakable subjects, we read only rarely of reactions to the unclothed male populations scattered around the world. Married women presumably weren't much concerned, having been introduced to the wonders of male anatomy by their husbands, but what effect would such sights have on maidens? Explorer Samuel Baker fumed at the idea that young, unmarried Alexine Tinne should see naked Nubians, but there is no record of what she thought. Woman of the world Mme Olympe d'Audouard couldn't get over how Englishwomen were utterly blasé about nudity among Egyptians; she had expected them to be outraged. In any case, mention of nudity was titillating and sure to capture the attention of reviewers and readers.[13]

The image of would-be lady authors, juggling parasols and notebooks as they clambered over ruins, provoked lampoons, including "Impulsia Gushington's" *Lispings from Low Latitudes* (1863).* A contemporary review called it "an exaggerated picture" of "those ladies who *will* travel where they have no business to travel, who *will* wear costumes which they have no business (in those latitudes) to

---

* This work has been assumed to be a parody of Lord Dufferin's book *Letters from High Latitudes* (1857) on his travels through Iceland, but he clearly wasn't too upset; he edited it, according to a publisher's ad.

Bell Smith Abroad (1855) by "Piatt" (Mrs. Louise Kirby) was one American woman's contribution to humorous travel literature.

wear; who *will* go 'unprotected;' who *will* choose their dragoman by physiognomy, as romance suggests, and not by advice of friends, as common sense would dictate."[15]

Spoofs are one thing, but the contributions of women such as Isabella Bird, Mary Kingsley and Anne Blunt to world exploration are unassailable. The Royal Scottish Geographical Society made Bird and Kingsley members, and the French elected Lydie Paschkoff and Ida Pfeiffer. But members of London's Royal Geographical Society turned their noses up at the thought, though they were obliged to accept twenty-two women in 1892, when they had unwittingly opened their doors to members of other societies. This door shut quickly, but not before Bird, Kate Marsden and May French Sheldon slipped in. George Curzon, who had met Bird on the Tigris in 1889 and seemed to hold a high opinion of her achievements, was especially hostile, saying: "Their sex and training render them equally unfitted for exploration, and the genus of professional female globetrotters with which America has lately familiarised us is one of the horrors of the latter end of the nineteenth century." Women were finally, irrevocably admitted to the society in 1913.[16]

Not all of the women in these pages were perfect heroines. Some, like Polish exile Ève Félinska, were squeamish to the point of ridiculousness; their fainting fits over the least little incidents must have given women a bad name all over the globe. And others, like Lydie Paschkoff, were so particular about their comforts that they lugged around clothing for all occasions and maids to help them dress; their entourages rivalled formidable desert caravans. Paschkoff was also vain, as were Carla Serena and Eliza Fay. A few women were bigoted to a degree inexcusable even for the time, though some of those—Isabella Bird, for example—overcame their prejudices.

Without self-imposed boundaries, a project such as this book would never be completed. I have reluctantly accepted that I cannot include everybody; I hope the reader will forgive me if a favourite traveller has been left out. In an effort to control the copious material, I have focused on women who distinguished themselves as travellers as opposed to those who travelled for a cause or an occupation. So, with a few exceptions, missionaries, governesses and settlers are not included.

I've also restricted the time period from the mid-seventeenth century to the end of the nineteenth century, as travel changed radically in the early 1900s. This means that many twentieth-century worthies, including Gertrude Bell, Freya Stark, Dervla Murphy and Ella Maillart, are excluded. I am also unable to delve deeply into individual lives, much as I'd like to. However, biographies of specific travellers, as well as their original books (many available as reprints), are well worth pursuing. My intent is not to go over the same ground covered by these books but, rather, to consider women travellers—both well-known and anonymous—in the context of travel of their time, especially through the illustrations and photographs of travel.

I have divided the book into regions to help the reader visualize the world around which women travelled. In this way, experiences that are shared by many—climbing the pyramids, for instance—are described from several points of view. The contrasts in opinions and approaches to travel reveal even more about the traveller than about the destination. But many of the wanderers here defy tidiness and pop up where you would least expect them. The girdlers of the world—Marianne North, Isabella Bird, Ida Pfeiffer and Lola Montez, for example—are particularly difficult to manage, a reflection, one might assume, of their lives in general.

The globe-trotting women in this book, along with hundreds, if not thousands, of unheralded anonymous ones, tore down boundaries, leaving as their legacy a world wide open for today's women. Their exploits beg the question; just when *was* a woman's place in the home?

Note: Except in quotations, I chose to spell place names according to current usage, using as my guide *Merriam Webster's Geographical Dictionary*. When *Webster's* let me down, I turned to the *Times Atlas of the World*, comprehensive edition. When both failed, I used the name as given by the original author. Where a name has changed completely—for example, Constantinople to Istanbul—I kept the original.

FOLLOWING PAGES:
Only an intrepid woman remains unfazed by the tumultuous crossing on a French steamer from Havre to Honfleur.
M. Biard, *ILN*, 19 September 1863: 285.

J. RUE SCRIBE,
PARIS.

Louis Vuitton

149, New Bond St.

OPPOSITE CONDUIT S.ᵗ

LONDON. W.

TELEGRAPHIC ADDRES

'VUITTON, LONDON.

Travelling Requisites

Diligences, Douaniers & Baedeker's

IN POSSESSION OF A MEASLY £60, Mary Godwin (later Shelley), her lover, Percy Bysshe Shelley, and her stepsister, Claire Clairmont, set out on foot from Paris in 1814, heading for Switzerland. They splurged on a donkey for Mary, who may have been pregnant at the time. In spite of warnings that Napoleon's ex-soldiers were wandering the countryside looking for women to assault, the travellers encountered no difficulties, except that Shelley sprained his ankle and commandeered the transport. It took them twelve days to get to Neuchatel, where they had their first wash since leaving Paris.[1]

If Godwin and Shelley had had more money, they could have bought or hired a coach and horses, a good choice for independence and for escaping the rabble. Wealthy Lady Elizabeth Craven, who travelled in the late 1700s, recommended that a friend "take as few servants as you can; drive your own Phaeton, and have another chaise for children or servants."[2]

Until the arrival of passenger train service,★ the run-of-the-mill traveller in Europe generally rode in a diligence, or stagecoach. These carriages, accompanied by postilions, or guides, travelled between stages, also known as *relais* or post houses. There, tired horses were exchanged for fresh ones and weary passengers could grab a meal or a few hours of sleep. Diligences were not noted for their comfort. Rapid travel was possible using this system, which was adopted throughout Europe by the mid-1700s. It was also available on limited routes in Russia, Mexico, North America, South Africa, India and the Middle East.

In addition to the diligence (six- to eight-seaters on four wheels), there were post-chaises (two- to

➤"When going by coach, avoid women, especially old women; they always want the best places."—E. S. Bates[4]

Advertisement for Louis Vuitton luggage showed how truly stylish some women travellers could be.
Orient-Pacific Line Guide, London: Sampson, Low, Marston, 1901, iv.

★ The first limited passenger runs began in Britain in 1825-26; Austria-Hungary followed a couple of years later, and by the mid-1850s most of Europe was well served by rail.[3]

four-seaters on four wheels), *char-à-bancs* (four-wheelers with benches) and *calèches* (four-seaters on two wheels). There were also various carts and city carriages.

Roads weren't up to today's standards. At best, a traveller would be regularly tossed into her neighbour's lap; at worst, accidents were tragically frequent. Lady Montagu would have been aware of this danger as she was driven in 1717 towards Constantinople (Istanbul):

> We passed by moonshine the frightful precipices that divide Bohemia from Saxony, at the bottom of which runs the river Elbe; but I cannot say that I had reason to fear drowning in it, being perfectly convinced that, in case of a tumble, it was utterly impossible to come alive to the bottom. In many places the road is so narrow, that I could not discern an inch of space between the wheels and the precipice . . . I perceived, by the bright light of the moon, our postilions nodding on horseback, while the horses were on a full gallop. Then indeed I thought it very convenient to call out to desire them to look where they were going.[5]

An artist's impression of a plucky young lady "Braving the Breeze" during the Channel crossing.
R. Taylor, *ILN*, 23 August 1884: 188.

Ferry boats were used for river crossings until bridges could be built, and crossing mountains meant going up and over until tunnels were blasted through. A significant improvement to the Lyon-Turin route to Italy was the opening of the Mont Cenis tunnel in 1871; before then, travellers had to ride, climb and/or be carried over a chain of mountains to the 2083-metre Alpine pass. Eliza Fay, who took this route in 1779, was surprised to see more Alps than she expected. Rising to the occasion, she wrote, "Being happily you know very courageous, I made light of all difficulties."[6] Her ascent was made on a mule intent on clinging to the cliff-side edge of the path, so she was relieved to transfer to a sedan chair for the descent. Luggage and even carriages had to be transported as well. Fay's post-chaise was partially dismantled and distributed onto the backs of several mules.

By no later than 1820, entrepreneurs had carved out a niche as early travel agents, known in France as *voiturins,* in Italy as *venturini* and in Germany as *Lohnkutscher.* They organized transport, lodging and meals for travellers and accompanied them for an agreed-upon sum. Generally, a number of people would share the arrangements, even if they weren't travelling together. Mary Shelley hired a *venturino* to take her from Milan to Geneva via the Simplon Pass in 1840. Her companions were three Scottish sisters, reinforcing her belief that Scottish women were most independent. Swiss *voiturins* reputedly swindled passengers once improvements to post roads increased traffic.[7]

"*The Opening of the Mont Cenis Tunnel; the town of Susa.*" *ILN,* 23 September 1871: 280.

Border formalities were the bane of travellers, though, according to Shelley, customs agents were partial to bribery everywhere but Germany. Most personal possessions, including books, linen and cutlery, were subject to duty or confiscation. Lady Craven had no time for borders: "It is ridiculous to hear the questions that are asked by the guards at the frontier towns: What is your name and quality? Are you married or single? Do you travel for pleasure or business?—It reminds me . . . of a traveller, who being asked his name, replied, Boo-hoo-hoo-hoo! 'Pray, Sir,' says the guard, 'how do you write it?' . . . It is impossible to answer such absurd questions with gravity."[8]

Customs agents were one type of robber; a more candid type was the *contrebandier,* or highwayman. In 1659, Lady Ann Fanshawe—protected by an escort of ten soldiers—went from Calais to Paris to meet her husband. They met a thieving troop of about fifty armed

soldiers, which her escort managed to turn back. Lady Ann asked the commander why his fellow soldiers had been threatening to rob them and was told, "Our pay is short, and we are forced to help ourselves this way, but we have this rule, that if we in a party guard any company, the rest never molest them, but let them pass free." Eighty years later, Lady Montagu noted that banditry was on the wane, and "you may cross the country with your purse in your hand."[9]

Customs didn't just operate at the borders we recognize today, for Europe was made up of fluidly incomprehensible kingdoms, territories and countries. Before 1848, the German confederation alone consisted of Austria-Hungary; the kingdoms of Bavaria, Württemburg, Saxony, Hanover and Prussia; and numerous duchies, principalities and free cities. Italy, after the 1815 Congress of Vienna until 1848, was really the kingdoms of Sardinia and the Two Sicilies, the Papal States and the duchies of Lucca and Tuscany. Control of Northern Italy was split by Austria and France.[10]

"Les Contrabandiers."
A medley of banditry
scenes at the French
frontier. O. Penguilly, n.d.

To add to the chaos, Europe, from the French Revolution (1789–99) until a second round of revolutions in 1848–49, was in continuous upheaval. From 1799 to 1815, Napoleon dragged France, Spain, Italy, England, Russia and Egypt into outright war. Later, the Franco-Prussian War of 1870-71 threw France and Germany into disarray, a conflict that in France was prolonged by the 1871 revolt of the Paris Commune. On other fronts, the Crimean War (1853-56) and the American Civil War (1861-65) were also disruptive, not just because of battles, but also because of the resulting disease, famine and social disorder, as well as the loss of transportation and lodging to military demands.

War did not discourage Lady Emmeline Stuart Wortley from

hauling her frail young daughter, Victoria, around the Continent in 1848, inciting her biographer to doubt that "such strenuous enterprises" were a fitting way to restore a child's health. Another undaunted traveller was china collector Lady Charlotte Schreiber, who defied warnings and rolled into Paris in a humble market cart in the midst of the Franco-Prussian War hunting for bargains. Louisa May Alcott, who had been a nurse during the American Civil War, did not let fighting stop her from accompanying an invalid friend to France in 1870, though she avoided hospitals.[11]

Guidebooks—in existence in a variety of forms for centuries—were invaluable for clearing up all the details of border formalities, available transportation, costs and hazards. One of the first printed English travel books was *Infomacõn for pylgrymes unto the holy londe* (1498). The 1700s saw a proliferation of guidebooks, including Tucker's *Instructions for Travellers* (1757) and Reichard's *Guide des voyageurs* (1793). Mariana Starke's *Travels on the Continent* (1820), later called *Travels in Europe,* became widely used and appeared in many editions. While exploring Naples in 1843, Mary Shelley relied on *Travels,* calling it "both accurate and well written." She also carried a copy of *Murray's Handbook for Travellers to the Continent,* the first edition of which appeared in 1836, catching his occasional errors with relish and adding her own hints.[12] *Murray's* grew rapidly to cover everywhere English-speakers might travel.

In 1839, Karl Baedeker published a German-language guide to the Rhine. He soon expanded his coverage, and his books became available in English and French. In France, Adolphe Joanne's guides, first published in 1841, along with his more portable *Guides diamants,* eventually became *Les Guides bleus.*

Another familiar name in travel was Cook's. Founded in 1841 as the brainchild of Thomas Cook, this tour company started with simple railway excursions around the British Isles and grew quickly to handle almost all a tourist's needs. It expanded to the Continent, with tours first to Paris, then to the Swiss Alps. In no time at all, Cook's was escorting travellers to every corner of the world. As far as I am aware, none of the women I discuss took advantage of its services, but it's safe to say that Cook's did more to encourage travel, especially among middle-class women, than any other tour company since.

TRAVELS IN EUROPE,

FOR THE USE OF

RAVELLERS ON THE CONTINENT,

AND LIKEWISE IN

THE ISLAND OF SICILY;

NOT COMPRISED IN ANY OF THE FORMER EDITIONS.

TO WHICH IS ADDED

AN ACCOUNT OF THE REMAINS OF ANCIENT ITALY,

AND ALSO OF THE ROADS LEADING TO THOSE REMAINS.

BY MARIANA STARKE.

The author of the following pages, being fully persuaded of the impossibility of writing an accurate account of the geography and antiquities of a country without having examined them herself; *and likewise feeling, from respect to the Public, an earnest wish not to be considered as an erroneous Guide, has lately visited almost every part of Italy, especially those parts which, in modern times, have been neglected by Travellers; and it may, perhaps, give* them *satisfaction to know that, throughout her recent excursions, she has always found the peasantry, mechanics, and tradesmen, well disposed toward their rulers, civil, orderly, and honest; insomuch that Travellers may, with safety, frequent the high roads, and likewise penetrate into the most secluded parts of the Alps and Apennine, without the slightest probability of being annoyed by popular tumults, or plundered by banditti.*—Mariana Starke[13]

PARIS,

PUBLISHED BY A. AND W. GALIGNANI AND Co.,

18, RUE VIVIENNE.

1839.

Europe
On Tour with the Fair Sex

IN 1785, ELIZABETH, LADY CRAVEN, stepped onto the Continent, expelled from England by her husband, the earl of Craven, for adulterous behaviour. Beautiful, vainglorious, cultivated and indiscreet, Lady Craven had married the soon-to-be earl at the age of sixteen, in 1767. Rumours of an extramarital liaison surfaced in 1773, and though her husband was not a paragon of fidelity himself, he found the fact that her tryst was reported in the press and that it was linked to a "famous house of carnal recreation" intolerable. He exiled her to the country but soon let her come back home. When she strayed again ten years later, he threw her out of the country.[1]

Lady Craven settled briefly at Versailles, where she met her future husband, the margrave of Anspach, but soon took to the road with Henry Vernon, a man with connections, money and free time. She and "cousin" Vernon trotted first to Italy and then to Austria, Poland and Russia and south through the Crimea to Constantinople. In October 1786, she returned to England and wrote *A Journey Through the Crimea to Constantinople* (1789).[2]

Five months later, she went to Anspach to be with the margrave but found French actress Mlle Clairon, the German lord's long-time mistress, in residence. She sent the actress packing, but in the meantime, the margrave was still married and ostensibly living with his wife, who, Lady Craven claimed, welcomed the new inamorata. The adulterous pair visited Italy through 1789–90 and married in Portugal in 1791, after both their spouses died. They toured Spain, rushed through revolution-torn France, then settled in England, where they entertained lavishly. After a period of immobility, they visited Paris and Vienna in 1801–1802.

In the year 747, English missionary St. Boniface was horrified to discover English harlots infesting the pilgrim route through France and Italy. He urged the clergy to forbid "matrons and veiled women" to make the pilgrimage to Rome, as too few managed to complete the trip without falling into a moral abyss. In spite of Boniface's outrage, the church was powerless to stop women from going to Rome, and some even reached the Holy Land. Clearly, women, even at this early date, were travelling in sufficient numbers to be noticed.[3]

Mme Anne-Louise-Germaine de Staël.
J. Champagne, n.d.

Lady Elizabeth Craven.
Craven, frontispiece.

Soon after the margrave's death early in 1806, Lady Craven was seen in the company of Louis XVIII and Ferdinand IV of Italy. She died in 1828 at the age of seventy-eight and was buried at the British cemetery at Naples.

Lady Craven, like Lady Montagu before her, was a trend-setter, who not only seemed to think that she had every right to travel but clearly had a good time doing so. Her well-publicized exploits may not have roused other women to pack their bags and leave home, but they certainly contributed to the growing conviction that women could travel as easily as men. Lady Craven's travels extended across Europe to Constantinople; most of the European travellers discussed here restricted their wanderings to specific countries.

FRANCE

Frances (Fanny) Trollope, in her book *Paris and the Parisians* (1836), summed up the attitude of the British towards France in her recounting of a conversation overheard at the port of Calais: "'What a dreadful smell!' said the uninitiated stranger, enveloping his nose in his pocket handkerchief. 'It is the smell of the continent, sir,' replied the man of experience."[4] For these travellers, the French countryside was a vexation to be got through to reach Paris or Italy.

French hotels were deemed to be the most wretched aspect of the journey. Lady Bury vented her frustration with them in 1814: "All the inns I have been in . . . are miserable; but they are quite good enough for the purposes of animal existence." Her usual complaint was lack of privacy, but at the Mulet Blanc in the town of Vienne, the rude landlord grossly overcharged her,

Europe. Philips' Handy Atlas, c. 1897.

telling her servant that "*les Anglois* [*sic*] had done him much mischief, and they should pay for it." Hotel charges seemed to vary with the traveller's ability to pay, provoking Lady Craven to advise sending a servant ahead to bargain for a fixed rate. Another disagreeable side of French hotels, for the gentle sex at least, was the *table d'hôte,* usually a great dining table at which all boarders sat and helped themselves pell-mell. Lady Montagu paid double at one hotel so she could have room service and avoid the savageries of feeding time.[5]

Once safely in Paris, a traveller could find endless diversions. A highlight of Russian princess Dashkov's stay in 1770 came when she joined the public tour at Versailles to gawk at Louis XV and his family on display eating dinner. An even more remarkable sight was the morgue. This melancholy place attracted Trollope, Eliza Fay and Emma Roberts, among others. Trollope asked, "Is there in any language a word that can raise so many shuddering sensations as '*La Morgue?*' Hatred, revenge, murder, are each terrible; but La Morgue outdoes them all in its power of

LEFT: *Lady Charlotte Bury.* Alexander Blaikley, Bury, vol. 1, frontispiece.

FACING PAGE: *Would you share a room with Laurence Sterne, author of* A Sentimental Journey through France and Italy? *This woman had no choice at a post inn in Savoy. Fortunately, she didn't know he had recently seduced a* fille de chambre *in Paris.*

T. H. Robinson 1897, facing p. 438.

"La Morgue: The Dead House of Paris."
Frank Leslie's, 6 February 1858: 156.

Lady Sydney Morgan.
S. Lover, Duyckinck, vol. 2, 167.

❧"[France] seemed to exist in order that Lady Morgan might write upon it."— William Davenport Adams[6]

bringing together in one syllable the abstract of whatever is most appalling in crime, poverty, despair, and death."[7]

Women churned out books about travel in France. Some, with titles like *A Spinster's Tour in France* and *A Lady's Walks in the South of France*, were penned by amateurs. But many, such as Matilda Betham Edwards (*A Year in Western France*, 1879) and the already mentioned Fanny Trollope, made a business of their writing. Another notable professional writer was Lady Sydney Morgan, who liked to claim that she was born in a boat heading for Dublin, though she refused to say in which year. Prolific and self-supporting, she apparently had an agreement with her husband, Sir Charles Morgan, that she could keep her earnings in her name, and she was free to travel as she wished. She and Sir Charles toured the Continent in 1815–16, collecting material for her book on France. She threw herself into the project, seeing everybody and doing everything. The eight-volume *France* (1817) was so successful that the publisher commissioned a similar work on Italy.[8]

ITALY

When we visit Italy, we become what the Italians were censured for being,—enjoyers of the beauties of nature, the elegance of art, the delights of climate, the recollections of the past, and the pleasures of society, without a thought beyond.—Mary Shelley[9]

In the 1840s, on her two trips to Italy, Mary Shelley crossed over three Alpine passes: the Simplon, the Splügen and the Brenner. Other passes she could have taken were Mont Cenis or the Great St. Bernard, or she could have gone by sea from Nice to Genoa or Livorno. There was something to be said against all of these options. The passes were physically demanding, and sea passages were frequently hindered by bad weather. But once she made it, Shelley, like most visitors, knew she had reached a very special destination, long celebrated by painters and writers.[10]

Of all the British travellers, Lord Byron, especially, had mythicized Italy; scores of young ladies read his "Ode to Venice" and dreamed of going there to meet the devastatingly romantic poet. His tragic death in 1824 reinforced the magic of the country he loved so well.

Mary Shelley. Romance of Mary Shelley, London: Bibliophile Society, 1907, facing p. 12.

Another promoter of things Italian, Byron's contemporary Mme Anne-Louise-Germaine de Staël, outspoken French intellectual, novelist and society darling, was the author of an unorthodox guide to Italy, the novel *Corinne, ou l'Italie (Corinne, or Italy)* (1807), a homage to the emotional power of Rome, Naples and Venice and, ostensibly, a love story between the beautiful Corinne, a paragon of Italian wit, and the restrained English lord Nelvil. Staël created in Corinne an unparalleled (though at times overblown and narcissistic) tour guide, who leads us through the Pantheon, Saint Peter's, the Forum and Pompeii. She breathes life into statues that would otherwise remain mute, she conducts us into the studios of great artists and she introduces us to the very idea of Italy. If we think we've seen Italy before we've read *Corinne*, chances are we've only been sleepwalking.

Staël was forced to travel; during the years of the French

Woodville

Revolution, she lived outside France as an émigrée, then, after Napoleon took power, as an exile. She, like Byron, was one of Europe's most popular tourist destinations, and for Englishwomen, especially, it was *de rigueur* to try to at least see her family home at Coppet, near Geneva, if they couldn't manage to visit her. Among those who made the pilgrimage was Marguerite, Lady Blessington, the author of *The Idler in Italy* (1839), who had also written *Conversations with Lord Byron* based on her friendship, made at Genoa, with the poet.

Blessington was an intelligent chronicler of English society in Naples. Residing there in splendour with her extravagant second husband, Charles John Gardiner, Earl of Blessington, from 1823 to 1826, she reigned over a brilliant circle of poets, scholars, astronomers and dandies. A frequent visitor was Sir William Gell, a noted archaeologist and one-time chamberlain to Princess Caroline. Gell conducted the Blessingtons around Pompeii and Herculaneum and amused them with his dry wit.★[11]

Blessington made the usual rounds to Vesuvius, to churches and to ruins, but her more unusual tourist activities included visiting the Grotto dei Cani, where, for the benefit of sightseers, a dog was exposed to noxious fumes until near death. She also viewed the remains of the recently deceased king of Naples and visited a lunatic asylum.

Although the title of her work implies that she was an indolent traveller, she never seems to have taken a breather from her strenuous tourist activities. She did, however, explain her choice of words: "Idleness, the besetting sin of this place, has taken possession of me. I shall journalize no more; but merely write down, whenever in the humour, what

"Travel, whatever else may be said of it, is one of the saddest pleasures in life. When you feel comfortable in a foreign city, it is because you have begun to make it your home; but passing though unknown countries, hearing a language you scarcely understand, seeing human faces unconnected with your past or future, is to know a solitude and isolation without respite and without dignity."—Mme de Staël, *Corinne, ou Italie.*[13]

"There is a plentiful supply of chairs before the doors of the principal *caffès*, and [the Italian ladies] sit and converse. It is not etiquette for a lady to enter a *caffè*, and they are shocked at the English women, who do not perceive the difference between eating their ice, or sipping their coffee, in the open Piazza, and entering the shop itself."
—Mary Shelley[14]

"The Tourist in Venice."
R. Caton Woodville, *ILN*,
8 October 1881: 361.

★ Gell's friend and fellow former chamberlain Keppel Craven was in Naples caring for his mother, Lady Craven, whom we have already met.[12]

Marguerite, Lady Blessington. H. Wright Smith, *Conversations with Lord Byron,* Boston: William Veazie, 1832, frontispiece.

occurs, or what I see. O the *dolce far niente* of an Italian life! who can resist its influence?—not I, at least."[15]

On their departure from Naples in 1826, the Blessingtons criss-crossed Italy, stayed in Florence for almost a year and eventually made their way to Paris, where they set themselves up in another splendid residence. But Lord Blessington keeled over and died shortly thereafter, leaving a mountain of debts. Lady Blessington's reputation also suffered. She became known as a squanderer, like her husband, of vast wealth, and as a paramour of her stepdaughter's husband, the inimitable rake Alfred, Count d'Orsay, with whom she returned to England. To pay off her own and d'Orsay's fabulously large debts, she wrote more travel books, including *The Idler in France* (1841). Although it's doubtful that she and her son-in-law were lovers, contemporary critics were censorious of her behaviour. Lady Blessington returned to Paris in May 1849, her belongings having been yanked from under her by the bailiff. She died a month later.[16]

In the meantime, Lady Sydney Morgan had also been writing a book on Italy, but whereas Blessington had settled in and taken her time, Lady Sydney had swept through, hastily scribbling notes. Nonetheless, of the result, *Italy* (1821), Byron, who had initially been scornful, wrote, "Her work is fearless and excellent . . . I wish she had fallen in with me." Mary Shelley, a friend of Lady Sydney's, wrote that "her book is dear to Italians," but it was placed on the papal index of prohibited works.[17]

Other notables who contributed to Italian travel accounts were Fanny Trollope (*A Visit to Italy,* 1843) and Frances Elliot. Although a reviewer of Elliot's *Diary of an Idle Woman in Italy* (1871) found little in it to praise, he did appreciate that "she confesses the gross rudeness, stupidity, and vulgarity of many travelling English, whose behaviour at Rome is too often shameful."[18]

Have first been to the Top 9th April 104

The ascent of Vesuvius was easy in the Cook's funicular, shown above, c. 1904, but eighty years earlier, when Lady Blessington went up, most tourists were carried partway in a chair:

Thomas Cook & Son postcard from Vesuvius, c. 1904.

Chairs, resembling those used in English farm-houses, and suspended to poles in a similar way to those that conveyed us across the mountains from Amalfi, were here ready for our use. But having tried one of them for a short time, I found the movement so disagreeable, owing to the chair-bearers slipping, and falling down at nearly every second step, in consequence of the lava and scoriae crumbling beneath their feet, that I preferred descending from my unstable altitude. Assisted by the arm . . . and holding by leather straps fastened round the waist of one of the guides who preceded me, I managed to ascend; but not without considerable difficulty and fatigue; being, like Sisyphus in his task, rolled back at each step.[19]

THE ALPS

The Alps attracted all kinds of travellers, not just the mountain-climbing variety. The rarefied air was considered a tonic for consumptives, the valleys were havens for natural history buffs and the countries sharing the Alps—Switzerland and Austria, especially—were thought to be safe and clean. Consequently, accounts of alpine journeys were a mixed bag of high-altitude rambles and rest cures.

Serious mountain climbers included Henriette d'Angeville, who, in 1838, planned her own ascent of Mont Blanc, coordinating twelve guides and porters to accompany her. Sisters Ellen and Anna Pigeon wrote in 1869 that they had been the first women to climb the Alps without a man. Elizabeth Le Blond, the author of *The High Alps in Winter: or, Mountaineering in Search of Health* (1883), chucked illness aside and tackled Mont Blanc, not once, but twice, in 1881. Lucy Walker, a pro who began her alpine career in 1858 and was to climb ninety-eight peaks in twenty-one years, became the first woman to climb the Matterhorn, in 1871.[20]

Elizabeth Le Blond. From a photo by J. Thomson, Dronsart, 371.

Dora d'Istria, born Helène Ghika in Bucharest, a talented linguist and historian, wrote of her ascent of the never-before-conquered Mönch, close to the Jungfrau, in *La Suisse allemande et l'ascension du Moench* (1856). She also wrote of her difficulties mastering men's clothing:

LEFT: *Dora d'Istria.* Cortambert, facing p. 267.

FACING PAGE: *"A victim of the Alps."* As women climbers watch in horror, a young man falls from the Doldenhorn, near Kandersteg. His descent was some six hundred metres. The article described how the numbers of tourists seeking alpine thrills had increased, as had fatal accidents. Fermo, La Tribuna illustrata, 26 July 1908: cover.

[I] dressed again in my masculine clothes, which I found difficult to get used to. I felt awkward; they hampered all my movements . . . I feared the guides would despair of me if they saw me stumble at each step. I was terribly humiliated and it took important reasons to prevent me from resuming my woman's dress. I finally came up with a quick solution. I made a parcel of my silk petticoat and my laced boots . . . so that I might make use

Amelia B. Edwards.
Photo by Kurtz, *Pharaohs, Fellahs and Explorers,* New York: Harper & Brothers, 1891, frontispiece.

of them should I become totally paralyzed by those beastly garments which I found so inconvenient.[21]

Amelia Edwards's account of her exploration of the Dolomites in the southeastern Tyrol, *Untrodden Peaks and Unfrequented Valleys* (1873), is that of an enthusiastic amateur. Edwards, who would later establish herself as an Egyptian scholar, started out July 1872 at Venice with a companion, "L," "L"'s delicate maid, "S," and a hopeless gentleman who was to serve as their courier, or escort. The ill-assorted group headed, first by train, then by carriage, for Cortina, near the Austrian border. There the courier decamped, horrified by the prospect of insalubrious Tyrolean inns and humble transport. Edwards observed, "Our vagabond tastes were too much for him; and he deserted us."[22]

In the hands of a suitable replacement, the party continued. They headquartered at Caprile, read the signatures of famous alpinists at a Predazzo inn, and in Pieve di Cadore were shown the bedroom where Titian was reputedly born. Edwards rejoiced in the absence of tour groups, though she thought the independent travellers she met, especially her fellow countrymen, were rude.

The women became, they were told, the first travellers to reach Sasso Bianco, the peak of Monte Pezza. It had been scorned by the Alpine Club as too ordinary but bypassed by ordinary travellers because it looked too difficult. Edwards, in awe of the idea of being the first to attain the summit, wrote, "Those words 'prima ascenzione' are Cabalistic, and haunt the memory strangely." A contemporary review called her book "pleasantly written with plenty of womanly anecdote and gossip, and with the usual information as to the fair travellers' married or unmarried condition," but pointed out that if, as she suggested, the Dolomites were not overtrampled by Cook's tourists, they soon would be, thanks to her.[23]

Except for the Alps, Germany and Austria—as well as their eastern neighbours Poland and Bohemia (the Czech Republic)—weren't considered powerfully attractive destinations, though Staël had given Germany a certain cachet with her book *En Allemagne* (1813), about her visit to that country and her friendships with Goethe and Schiller. Austria was dismissed by one writer with a curt "[it's] not a country about which much is unknown, nor are the British thirsting for information about it," in a review of Lizzie Eden's book, *My Holiday in Austria* (1869).[24]

On her monumental spin through Europe, Lady Craven remarked that "Germans are civil if you pass through their countries; but if you reside in them, they imagine you have a plan—a scheme—and nothing can divest them of the idea." In 1837, Lady Frances Londonderry found much to please her in Berlin and Dresden, especially the museums, but she pronounced all German cooking "poisonous."[25]

The spas, however, were a great attraction. Marienbad, Baden-Baden and Kissingen swarmed with visitors looking for water cures. If the baths weren't sufficient entertainment, travellers could try learning German or, failing that, enjoy the casinos.

"Sightseeing: A Swiss Morgue." Not content with limiting their days to hikes, ladies also viewed frozen corpses, which had been displayed for the purposes of identification. Side-Lights on English Society by E. C. Grenville-Murray, London: Vizetelly, 1883, 75.

SPAIN *and* PORTUGAL

Spain and Portugal were considered exotic destinations, but travel there was hampered by cholera epidemics, brigand-infested roads and indigestible food. (Garlic and oil were especially abhorred by the English.) None of these drawbacks deterred Lady Ann Fanshawe, a frequent and early visitor to the Iberian Peninsula. She and her husband, Sir Richard, England's ambassador to Spain, lived there in 1647, 1662 and 1664. By the standards of the time, the Fanshawes travelled in luxury. They were wined and dined by Europe's elite, but getting to these sumptuous affairs entailed

inconvenience and danger both on land and at sea. Of a dicey moment in 1650, when a Turkish pirate ship approached hers, Lady Ann wrote:

> We believed we should all be carried away slaves, for [the Dutch captain] had so loaden his ship with goods for Spaine that his guns were useless, though the ship carried 60 guns. He called for brandy, and after he had well drunken and all his men, which were neare 200, he called for armes and cleared the deck as well as he could, resolving to fight rather than lose his ship that was worth 30000lb. This was sad for us passengers, but my husband bid us to be sure to keepe in the cabine and not appear (no woman), which would make the Turks think we were a man of war; but if they saw women, they would take us for merchants and boord us . . . This beast captain had locked me up in the cabine. I knocked and called long to no purpose, untill at length a cabine boy came and opened the doore. I, all in tears, desired him to be so good as to give me his blew throm cap he wore and his tarred coat, which he did, and I gave him half a crown, and putting them on and flinging away my night's clothes, I crept up softly and stood upon the deck by my husband's side as free from sickness and fear as, I confess, from discretion.[26]

Robbers, shipwrecks and drunken sailors were just part of the difficulties; Lady Ann was also frequently pregnant and had, depending on the source, between fourteen and eighteen babies, few of whom survived.[27]

ABOVE: *Ann, Lady Fanshawe*. Fiesenger, n.d.

FACING PAGE: *Vermillion Tower at the Alhambra in Granada, Spain*. Drawing by David Roberts, engraving by Freebairn, *Jennings Landscape Annual for 1835*, or *The Tourist in Spain*, by Thomas Roscoe, London: Robert Jennings, 1835.

Lady Ann loved Spain. She thought the food superior to English food (though admitted finding anything decent was a problem for those without money), the manners of the men impeccable, the beauty of the women remarkable, and "when they travell they are the most jolly people in the world, dealing their provisions of all sorts to every person they meet, when they are eating."[28]

In June 1666, when Sir Richard was struck with ague and died, the Spanish queen, Anne, invited Lady Ann to stay in Spain and offered a generous pension, but she refused, risking instead a future of poverty in England.

Lady Ann's memoirs were not published until 1829. In the meantime, one of the first women to publish a book of travel to Spain was unfortunately having her readers on. *Travels into Spain [etc.]* (1691) by Marie-Catherine Le Jumel de Barneville, baronne d'Aulnoy, was a spicy read, and Aulnoy was wildly popular in her age, best known for her fairy tales *La Chatte blanche* and *L'Oiseau bleu,* and for her caustic portrayals of seventeenth-century court life.

Travels into Spain begins with Aulnoy heading south from Bayonne to Madrid and recording her observations of Spanish mores and customs through anecdotes learned from fellow travellers. The travelogue has an Arabian Nights quality, with each stop adding a cautionary tale of morality, danger or intrigue. Interspersed are vignettes of conniving customs agents and innkeepers as well as commentary on bullfights, cuisine and the hazards of winter travel. The storytelling raised suspicions about the credibility of her trip, convincing at least one editor that her Spanish adventures were fictional and that most of her book was cribbed from existing writings.[29]

Aulnoy's personal life was controversial. Around age sixteen she married the debauched Baron d'Aulnoy, and three years later, with the help of her mother and others, had him thrown into the Bastille on a charge of treason. He proved his innocence, two gentlemen lost their heads over the incident and Aulnoy reputedly fled to England and then Spain. She resurfaced in Paris around 1690 and became one of the bright lights of that city's literary scene.[30]

The background of traveller Janet Schaw is even sketchier, but of the credibility of her account there's no doubt. Schaw, at the time of her visit to Portugal in 1775, had just left the Carolinas to escape the pending American War of Independence and was returning to her home in Scotland via the *George*. She arrived at the port of Setúbal, but before she could disembark for a brief visit to Lisbon, the boat was boarded by customs officers intent on confiscating tobacco, followed by health officers and then by a representative of the Inquisition. This last visitor terrified her, even though the holy representative turned out to be a young and unassuming priest. She; her ward, Fanny Rutherfurd; and fellow passenger Archibald Neilson—who posed as Schaw's husband, for convenience' sake—travelled by calèche and mule to Lisbon, but they were arrested by government agents, in a ruse to collect money, as they tried to cross the Tagus River.

Schaw's good humour faltered at the next stage of the trip:

> The Night was cold and a drizling [*sic*] rain had come on. It was also so dark, that I lost all the pleasure I hoped for on the Tagus. Tho' we had hired the boat entirely, it was half full of dead hogs, fish and a variety of articles for Market, and we were hardly set off from the shore, when the crew began chanting their Vespers, and had the dead swine which lay by them joined their grunts to the concert, it could not have rendered it more disagreeable.[31]

In Lisbon, a doctor told her that the British "loved mightily to be buried at Lisbon, as they seldom come there, till just ready to step into the grave."[32] It is not known when or if Janet Schaw returned to Scotland. Her unpublished letters were not discovered until 1921.

Travel in Iberia wasn't much better in the nineteenth century. Lisbon's ubiquitous filth crushed poet Marianne Baillie, who declared, "It has such an overpowering effect on my nerves, that I have sometimes found it impossible to refrain from absolute tears of disgust."[33]

Inns, except in major centres such as Madrid, were basic. And in Lisbon, even luxury hotels had drawbacks. In 1867, Isabel and Richard Burton stayed at the regal Braganza, where their room was already occupied by three-inch-long cockroaches, the sight of which catapulted Isabel onto a chair, screaming. When Richard said sarcastically, "I suppose you think you look very pretty and interesting," she collected herself, jumped back onto the floor and proceeded to slaughter the blighters. In two hours, she murdered ninety-seven of them. The Burtons were given another room, and, a couple of days later, they laughed upon hearing the next guest, Lady Lytton, scream. The room of another guest, Emmeline Wortley, was constantly filled with smoke from the chimney stacks of the houses below.[34]

Squalor was one of Frances Elliot's targets in *Diary of an Idle Woman in Spain* (1884). Like her other books, it has a breezy "seen

it all, done it all" tone, but her descriptions of street scenes, museums and people are sharp and witty, if not snide. For her
exhaustive and exhausting tour of Madrid, Seville, Cadiz, Malaga,
Cordoba, Valencia, Alicante, Granada and Salamanca, she travelled
by train, omnibus and diligence; survived a flood en route to
Cordoba; and suffered odious hotels everywhere.

Her advice for dealing with train stations was practical: "If you
do not wish to have your possessions ransacked, you must fee a
sour-faced official, who, with greedy eyes and wiry fingers, already
grasps the cords. Quick, quick! Out with your purse and settle it!"
Her first reaction to Seville—"Oh dear! It is so ugly. Take it all in
all, I never saw an uglier town. It does seem hard to have
come so far for this!"—was softened by a lengthy stay.
Malaga could not redeem itself: "A horrible place! I
should like to swear! A beastly place! I *will* swear! . . .
All sun, dirt, traffic, merchant ships, bad smells,
mulebells, rattling wheels, screams, shouts, ugliness
and dust!"[35]

Frances Elliot. From a photo by
Maull and Fox, Dronsart, 257.

Fellow travellers fared no better; of the tourist
inundation of the Alhambra, Elliot wrote, "You
marvel whence they all come from, but they swarm.
Some rushing in apparently just as they land, bedrag-
gled and travel-stained, bonnets awry, great-coats and
travelling caps; others in jaunty toilettes of red and
green, with cock's feathers to match; long dresses,
muddy and trailing on the delicate marble squares, and all loud-
voiced and with vindictive airs of self-appropriation."[36]

SCANDINAVIA

In her book *Letters Written during a Short Residence in Sweden,
Norway, and Denmark* (1796), Mary Wollstonecraft advised that
"travellers who require that every nation should resemble their
native country, had better stay home." One hundred years later,
Baedeker's echoed her sentiments, warning that travellers who "are
addicted to luxurious hotels . . . and other fashionable resorts will
not find Norway to their taste." Wollstonecraft, Mary Shelley's
mother, had travelled to Scandinavia to try to salvage the ship of
her unfaithful lover Gilbert Imlay, with its smuggled load of silver.
She was also trying to salvage something of their relationship. The

edited correspondence in her book is intelligent, calm, leisurely paced and reflective. It is, however, a far cry from a more recently published collection of Wollstonecraft's personal letters, which reveal the true pitfalls of travel: loneliness, insecurity and fear, reinforcing her achievement in traversing this wild landscape.[37]

Scandinavia was not considered much of a tourist destination in 1836 either, when Lady Frances Anne Londonderry, along with her husband and son, set out to visit St. Petersburg via Denmark and Sweden. The former British ambassador to Vienna, Lord Londonderry had been offered the ambassadorship to Russia but was forced to decline in the face of widespread opposition. The couple decided to go to St. Petersburg anyway, in an unofficial capacity.[38]

They were old travel hands, having honed their skills between London, Vienna and northern Italy. Lady Londonderry kept a journal of the trip, generally a record of her almost daily burdens of picking out what to wear to this ball or that dinner. Of the many cities they passed through, Stockholm pleased her most, even though their hotel room was merely a passage through which everyone tromped. The museum earned a special mention: "The *Musée* . . . [is] shown by a civil little man who seems very proud of his charge and wholly unconscious that it is one mass of rubbish." And, in spite of the fact that she herself was described as "dumpy, rum-shaped and rum-faced," she found Swedish ladies, like their counterparts throughout northern Europe, to be plain and prone to wearing "peculiarly unbecoming" outfits.[39]

Mary Wollstonecraft.
A.L. Merritt, in *Mary Wollstonecraft*, London: C. Kegan Paul, 1879, frontispiece.

GREAT BRITAIN

Before journeying to England, Princess Catherine Vorontsov Dashkov, whom we previously met gazing at the sight of Louis XV dining, became involved in the assassination of Russian emperor Peter III. In 1762, Peter's wife, Catherine the Great, with a little help from her friends, had seized the Russian throne from him, then had him killed. Mixed up in this scheme, possibly unwittingly, was the twenty-six-year-old Dashkov, one of Catherine's ladies-in-waiting. When she and her two children toured Europe in 1769 (she had been widowed five years earlier), her notoriety had preceded her and gave her an entrée into the best society, where she met the likes of writers Horace Walpole and Denis Diderot.[40]

Dashkov travelled to Berlin, London and through France, and her penchant for trouble making took a lighter turn at the stately Hôtel de Russie in Danzig (Gdánsk), where she was shocked "at seeing in the main room two pictures representing two battles lost by the Russian troops, who were shown wounded, dying, or standing on their knees before the victorious Prussian[s]." The Russian chargé d'affaires was unwilling to ask that the paintings be destroyed, so Dashkov and some fellow Russians ordered a few tubes of oil paint, locked themselves into the room and "made the troops exchange their uniforms. The Prussians—supposed to be victors in the two battles—became Russians, and the defeated were given Prussian uniforms."[41]At Geneva she met Voltaire and became a regular visitor at his deathbed. She returned to Russia in December 1771, but she was off again in 1776, when she took her children to Edinburgh, having enrolled her son in the university. By the end of his two-year term, she was suffering from ill health and poverty, but, intent on continuing her travels, she borrowed £2000, then visited Ireland, London and the Continent. After an extensive tour of Italy, she returned to St. Petersburg in 1782, with a collection of some fifteen thousand fossils, minerals and botanical specimens. This tour marked the end of Dashkov's travels; she became director of the Academy of Sciences and president of the Academy of Russian Languages.

We can read so much of what British women thought of Europe that it's a pleasure to find out what European women thought of Britain, though Johanna Schopenhauer, a German Anglophile, was not as critical as her British counterparts. She was a polyglot, a novelist, the mother of the philosopher Arthur, a friend of Goethe and a contemporary of Staël.

Her diaries, kept from 1803 to 1805, were first published as *Reise nach England.* They follow Schopenhauer and her husband's haphazard itinerary through England and Scotland's estates and parks. She visited Peak Caves near Chatsworth, where her guide—possibly mistaking her group for French tourists—pretended to toss one of them into its depths. Becoming overly caught up with sightseeing, she pocketed a souvenir hunk of coal from a mine, then came to her senses when refused entry to the Carron Iron Works: "It is a fact that while travelling one tends to look at things just because they happen to be there . . . One is inspired merely by some sense of duty, and often wishes afterwards that one had not taken the trouble."[42]

She commented on everything, and British ladies, who were always the first to point out how quickly beautiful young foreign women aged, would have been taken down a peg by this remark: "The English country-girls and young women are generally fine figures, though with age they tend to grow fat."[43]

Schopenhauer's husband died in 1806, possibly from suicide. Her other travel books, *Reise von Paris* and *Ausflug an den Niederrhein und nach Belgien im Jahr 1828,* were based on travels she made before and after his death.

Although Europe could serve up its share of bugs, bandits and bad hotels, many women saw it as a kind of proving grounds, where they could hone their skills as travellers in anticipation of even greater adventure. By the early nineteenth century, women had more than adequately shown that they were as able travellers as any man, and with delight and determination, they set their sights on the lands beyond.

Russia
Realizing the Unrealizable

WHEN LADY LONDONDERRY and her husband raced along the superbly engineered post road from St. Petersburg and Moscow in 1836, she was impressed. The road was flat and macadamized for its entire length, allowing a post-chaise or sled to complete the journey in only five days. She marvelled at the architecture of the inns along the way. At one inn, she thought the grand room she was given—with its parquet floor, sumptuous hangings and high, ornate ceiling—magnificent. But as soon as she sat down, she felt sharp pinpricks on her backside and legs, followed by unbearable itching. As she scratched and squirmed, thousands of tiny black projectiles landed on her skirts, and her skin erupted into red blotches. She'd become as infested with fleas and bugs as the room itself. Finding vermin-free accommodation was so difficult that the Russian empress should have known better when she asked Londonderry why her skin was so red.[1]

> "In Russia, travelling is not, as elsewhere, synonymous with seeing new sights."—Adèle Hommaire de Hell[2]

For European travellers, Russia was a vast unknown, a land of fantasy ice palaces, populated by tall, bearded Cossacks. But a Russian tour took a great commitment of time and resources, and almost everyone who went was obliged to endure at least one punishing winter. The Londonderrys travelled in luxury; for those without the protection of money and contacts, getting about was a grim proposition. And whereas St. Petersburg and Moscow were challenging, Siberia was almost unimaginable.

SIBERIA

What drove women to Siberia? Some went on missions, some for work; few viewed it as a pleasure jaunt. But Polish political exile Ève Félinska, for one, did not go by choice. She was shipped from the Ukraine to Siberia in March 1839, by a series of sleds that operated in relays, the same way as diligences. Of the exhausting trip she wrote, "One barely arrived before setting off

Carla Serena returning from the monastery of Bedia, in the Caucasus. Y. Pranishnikof, *Tour du monde* 43, 1882: 381.

The rescue of Ève Félinska. Durand-Brager, *Tour du monde* 6, 1862: 221.

again, and my infernal team followed its course across the snowy abyss. Neither the elements, nor the obstacles, nor the dangers could moderate the ardour of the postilions: a superhuman force seemed to push us onward."[3] Accompanied by her "jailer," as she called him, and two other *exilées,* she headed east as the snow melted and the route disintegrated into mud. After a month on the road, they reached Tobolsk in Western Siberia, where they remained until the river Irtysh, raging from spring meltwater, subsided.

The next stage entailed a two-week sail downriver, but only days after getting underway, Félinska imprudently sat in a flimsy lifeboat, which was set adrift by a stiff breeze. Terror of being parted from the boat—what another exile might have considered a chance to escape—paralyzed her. She was hauled, fainting, onto the deck by a quick-thinking flour merchant. She arrived at her final destination, Berezovo, without further incident at the end of May and settled in, modestly but comfortably housed. Félinska was eventually allowed to return to her family.

French violoncellist Lise Cristiani also braved Siberia, but as a musician, not an exile. Cristiani had established herself as a virtuoso

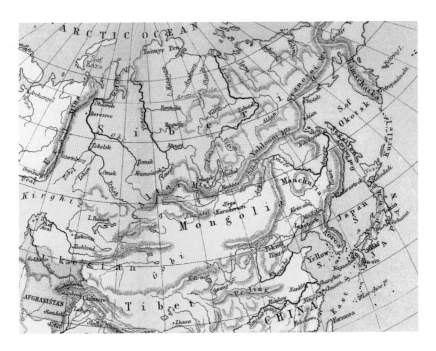

in Scandinavia, then went to St. Petersburg in 1849 to "make her fortune."[4] The move was a mistake; St. Petersburg, in mourning from a death at court, had become a ghost town, so she packed up and went east, accompanied by her Stradivarius, a Russian maid and a German pianist who doubled as her guardian.

Siberia. Philips' Handy Atlas, c. 1897.

Her account, published in the *Tour du monde* in 1863, began at Irkutsk, capital of Eastern Siberia. From there she travelled to the border town of Kyakhta, which had a sizable Chinese population. The Chinese were hospitable and curious, and held a grand dinner in her honour. She was asked dozens of questions by her host, the leading one why she was there. She had no idea if he believed that she only wanted to see what the frontier was like. She was taken to see the quarter's temple and afterwards attended a play, in which she was able to discern more than a touch of indecency, even though she didn't know a word of Chinese.

Lise Cristiani and her Stradivarius. After Couture, *Tour du monde 7*, 1863: 384.

Cristiani was also invited to the caravan of a local nomadic tribe. Escorted by a convoy of three hundred horsemen dressed in colourful satin robes, she crossed the steppes to the encampment, where she was given a dinner of roasted sheep and champagne. From there she visited a Tibetan Buddhist temple. The next stop, Yakutsk, was a real "hole," though men politely removed their hats as they passed her lodgings.[5]

The three travellers then went to Kamchatka, as far east as they could go. By mid-October they were back on the mainland, travelling west on horseback through difficult terrain. Cristiani became lost; fortunately, an army messenger, who happened to be passing, let her follow him but warned he would not stop if she fell behind. She struggled unsuccessfully to keep up, and as he disappeared she heard him remind her of his warning. Exhausted, she dropped her reins, ready to leave her fate to her horse's good sense, when the messenger returned. Whether he pitied her or her horse she had no idea, but she managed to make it to the next relay and rejoin her party.

By the end of the year, she had given over forty concerts, and the difficult journey had stolen all of her energy. She went to the Caucasus to recuperate but succumbed to cholera in October 1853.

Siberia's grim reputation did not stop British nurse and author of *On Sledge and Horseback to Outcast Siberian Lepers* (1893) Kate Marsden from going to Yakutsk to find a herb that supposedly cured leprosy. No stranger to trying conditions, the deeply religious Marsden had been a nurse in the Russo-Turkish War of 1877–78 and had visited Jerusalem and Constantinople to learn more about leprosy. She arrived in Moscow, inadequately dressed, in December 1890. Unhampered by her ignorance of Russian, she gained official approval for her visit. She and her friend Ada Field, who accompanied her partway, set about preparing for departure:

> In a few weeks everything was ready for this perilous, long, and unknown journey. What am I saying—a perilous journey?—nay, some people said I was going to take a "pleasure trip." So let it be. I plead guilty to the soft impeachment on the one condition that all ladies who give this seductive term to my journey will undertake to start from the vicinity of Moscow on the first of February next year.[6]

Marsden packed up stores of food, including some eighteen kilograms of plum pudding, reasoning it would keep well, and besides, she liked it. Her get-up consisted of Jaeger clothing: a down-filled ulster covered by a sheepskin coat covered by a reindeer-skin cloak in which she was unable to bend or to manoeuvre herself into a sleigh.

Despite the padding, the sleigh rides left her feeling "more like a battered old log of mahogany than a gently-nurtured Englishwoman."[7] And the Russian inns introduced her to odours and wildlife in the

Kate Marsden. "I wish to thank you for having persuaded me to wear Jaeger Clothing. Humanly speaking I owe my life to that and not taking stimulants; and I really believe that no woman could have gone through all my dangers, privations and difficulties without both of these aids to health." (Advertisement) Marsden, facing p. 15.

➤"Of course, it was quite natural for the gentlemen to remark that, like most of my sex, I wanted to get at the end of the journey before setting off."—Kate Marsden[8]

form of vermin that she had never dared imagine. At Omsk, Field turned back because of ill health. Marsden's mind began playing tricks on her, colouring harmless situations with menacing overtones, but she eventually accustomed herself to isolation and dependence on strangers. At rest stops, she visited prisons and handed out religious tracts.

When she finally reached Yakutsk in the spring, one of her first visits was with the local bishop, who showed her the herb she sought, though he hadn't heard of its efficacy against leprosy. In late June, she and an escort set off to find lepers. She dressed in knee-length trousers to facilitate riding astride, "because no woman could ride on a lady's saddle for three thousand versts."★[9] She also wore a deerstalker and a long-sleeved jacket with a Red Cross band on one arm. A gun and a whip completed the outfit.

Kate Marsden.
From a photograph by Renard of Moscow,
Dronsart, 401.

The trip was a tedious and boggy circuit through torrential rains or fierce heat. Unable to change clothes or bathe, she was astonished that neither she nor her companions caught colds. Their supplies spoiled quickly, so they had to buy food where they could. She found her poor and neglected lepers, crowded together in yurts, but the help she could give was negligible.

After a harrowing ride through a forest, where the earth under the surface of the ground was on fire, shooting up eerie flames around the travellers, she gave in to exhaustion. "I had never been on a horse before . . . and after all these weeks of riding on a hard saddle, with little sleep and food, and all the perils and alarms of the journey—well, it was time, perhaps the reader may think, that I did get exhausted." Her fears that she was developing an "internal malady" came to pass, and she spent the remainder of the trip in great pain.[10]

She made it back to Yakutsk having learned nothing more about the herb but with firm ideas about how to improve lepers' lives. She then returned, in the approaching winter, to Moscow. Amy Field met up with her at Tyumen, and the two travelled on together. Marsden returned to England in the spring of 1892.

★ A verst equals 1.067 kilometres or 0.6629 miles.

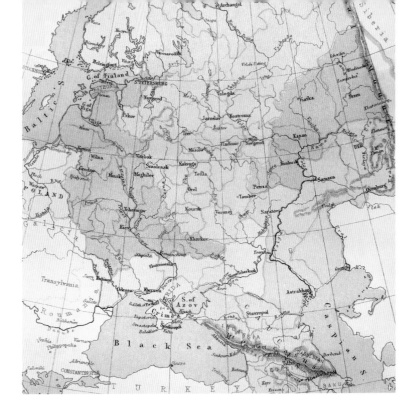

Western Russia.
Philips' Handy Atlas, c. 1897.

The CRIMEA *and the* CAUCASUS

Travellers who did not fancy Siberia could visit Southern Russia. Mrs. Maria Guthrie, the "acting directress of the Russian Imperial Convent,"[11] left St. Petersburg in 1795 for the Black Sea, in a futile effort to improve her health. Given the difficult travel conditions, she chose an odd destination for such a purpose. Her experiences were published in *A Tour, Performed in the Years 1795–6, Through the Taurida, or Crimea [etc.]* (1802), as a series of undated letters to her antiquities-obsessed husband, Dr. Matthew Guthrie, an army physician and counsellor to Alexander I.

Guthrie's letters, originally in French, were translated and heavily edited by her husband after her death. Most read like an academic history sprinkled with womanly touches. In one of her letters, she gives her reasons for writing of scholarly concerns. "Pray remember," she wrote, "that I intend to put a great deal of method into my Tour, just to punish you men for your sneer at *the charming disorder that must reign in the narrative of a female traveller.*"[12] Few personal details emerge; her wanderings may have been apocryphal, a device created by Matthew Guthrie as a means of capturing a wider audience for his own dry compositions.

Notwithstanding my ignorance of science, I felt that in sharing my husband's toils, I was in some sort a partner in his learned researches, and that I too, like him, had my claims upon the Caspian.—Adèle Hommaire de Hell[13]

Adèle Hommaire de Hell was very much the author of her own work, even though her writing bore her husband's name. *Travels in the Steppes of the Caspian Sea* (1847) by Xavier Hommaire de Hell, at the time considered a definitive study of the Crimea and the Caucasus, was cowritten by Adèle.

Adèle Hommaire de Hell.
E. Lefebure, Cortambert, frontispiece.

The account covered the years between 1838 and 1845, when the Hommaires and their young son travelled throughout Southern Russia. Her writing is filled with moments of pure magic; her description of traversing the Caucasian steppes in the escort of wild Cossacks is breathtaking. But her euphoria was never far from being crushed by doses of real danger. While riding through an especially thick patch of fog, she was told of a Polish woman who had been ambushed the previous year by Circassians. Her escort and servants were "massacred or dispersed, her carriage was rifled, and she herself was carried off and never heard of again." No sooner had this story been related when the fog cleared to reveal a group of Circassians standing before them. Adèle shrieked; she was assured that they were friendly but watched with suspicion as they filed past, certain they'd pounce and use the "damasked poniards [that] glittered beneath their black bourkas."[14] Aside from the threat of abduction, travel was difficult at the best of times. Here she sums up what kept her going, even in trying circumstances:

> The novelty of my sensations, and the secret pleasure of escaping for awhile from the round of prescribed habits that make up the chief part of civilised life, banished from my mind every sombre thought. The excursion was an experimental glimpse of those natural ways of life which are no longer possible in our thickly-peopled lands; . . . a nomade [*sic*] existence no longer seemed to me so absurd or wearisome as I had supposed it to be.[15]

At the Crimean village of Karolez, Adèle managed to meet the seldom-viewed and legendarily beautiful Princess Adel Bey. She let no detail of her visit escape, committing to memory such things as the princess's odd way of blackening her eyelids so that the paint met on the bridge of her nose. She and the princess, whose beauty exceeded her expectations, scrutinized each other closely. "What would I not have given to know the result of her purely feminine analysis of my appearance! ... [I] presented myself before her in male attire, which must have given her a strange notion of the fashions of Europe."[16]

Her masculine costume impressed another Tartar woman:

> I passed in front of a house in the large balcony of which there were three veiled women. Just as I passed beneath the balcony I slackened my horse's pace and made some friendly signals to them, whereupon, one of them, and I make no doubt the prettiest, repeatedly kissed a large bouquet of lily of the valley she held, and threw it to me so adroitly that it fell into my hand. Delighted with the present, I hastened up to my companions and showed it to them; but they were all malicious enough to assure me that the gift had been addressed not to myself but to my clothes.[17]

At Oulou Ouzen, north of Yalta, she met Mlle Jacquemart, an eccentric Frenchwoman who lived in isolation nearby. Jacquemart, a former governess who had achieved fame through her beauty and wit, was the target of thieves, so she slept with a brace of pistols. One attempt on her life left her with a fractured skull.

The Hommaires left the Crimea in 1845, then returned again the next year. Xavier died at Isfahan in 1849 at the age of thirty-six. Adèle continued to roam and wrote several more books on travel.[18]

Another woman traveller to the Crimea was Jamaican Mary Seacole. That this brown-skinned daughter of a Scottish officer and a freeborn black boarding-house keeper should end up running a hotel near Balaclava during the Crimean War is anything but logical. According to her own account, *Wonderful Adventures of Mrs. Seacole in Many Lands* (1857), she found her vocation early as an entrepreneur and a medic, nursing her mother's guests when they came down with cholera or yellow fever.

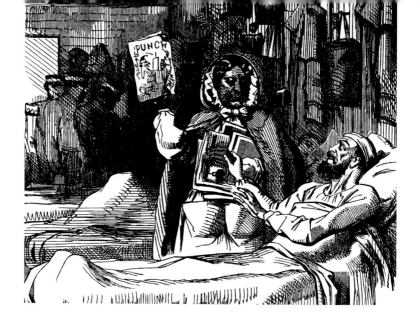

"All my life long I have followed the impulse which led me to be up and doing; and so far from resting idle anywhere, I have never wanted inclination to rove, nor will powerful enough to find a way to carry out my wishes . . . These qualities have led me into many countries, and brought me into some strange and amusing adventures . . . Some people, indeed, have called me quite a female Ulysses. I believe that they intended it as a compliment; but from my experience of the Greeks, I do not consider it a very flattering one."—Mary Seacole[19]

She married the sickly Mr. Seacole, cared for him until he expired, then, at the height of the California gold rush, coincident with a cholera outbreak in Jamaica, hightailed it to the Isthmus of Panama. A few years later, when she heard of the conflict in the Crimea, she couldn't get there fast enough, for, as she declared, "no sooner had I heard of war somewhere, than I longed to witness it."[20] She arrived in London in the autumn of 1854, but her applications to the war office and to Florence Nightingale's representatives to be taken on as a nurse were met with amusement.

Undaunted, she left in January 1855 for Balaclava and established the British Hotel in nearby Spring Hill. War was exciting; bombardments and confrontations surrounded her; she braved whizzing shells to take refreshments out to the battlefields, making her, almost certainly, the first woman caterer to get behind the lines at Sevastopol. Rats, thieves, freezing temperatures and occasional murders were no match for Seacole, but the 1856 armistice brought mixed feelings, as she had to sell out at a loss. The *Illustrated London News* pictured a crowd waiting to be evacuated; among them was Seacole, dressed in plaid, her back to us. The paper commented that she was "very much liked, and, from all accounts did a great deal of good." A year later, Punch was pleading with readers to spare a guinea to keep her from destitution.[21]

Between 1876 and 1878, Italian traveller Mme Carla Serena explored the Caucasus from the Black Sea to the Caspian; her book, *De la Baltique à la Caspienne* (1881), was the result not only of these travels but of her perpetual wanderings through Europe and the Middle East. She also had several articles published in the *Tour du monde* (1881–84). Her reasons for travelling were not revealed, and she avowed in *De la Baltique* a reluctance to focus on herself, a modesty not evident in her writing.

Serena travelled on horseback with a caravan that brought with it all necessities, as no inns or provisions were to be found along the way. She was welcomed into many homes, sharing with impoverished villagers their weddings and, as the region was as volatile then as it is now, memorials for the dead. For all the hospitality, she bemoaned one inescapable handicap: she couldn't speak a word of the local language. Rather than learn it, however, she endured three months of silence, a "difficult privation for a woman," she admitted.[22]

Carla Serena.
Dronsart, 79.

She managed to obtain permission to go to Abkhazia from an official who told her that her "heroism bordered on madness."[23] Accompanied by a *tchapar,* or guide, she stayed in private homes or at *doukans*—part inns, part supply depots—where she was forced to hide her disgust at being served by barefoot locals dressed in filthy rags.

Publication of her work was delayed by a lack of pictures, so she returned to the Caucasus in November 1881. Because photographers shrank from the dangerous region, she took the photographs herself, even though she had never used a camera and had neglected to try it out before she left. Miraculously, she was successful, developing her photographs in makeshift darkrooms along the way. When she returned to Europe, a celebrated geologist who had spent many years in the Caucasus congratulated her on her trip, saying, "You have realized the unrealizable!"[24]

The Middle East
Desert Queens

THE MIDDLE EAST GAVE EUROPEAN WOMEN a chance to discover a never-before-dreamed-of advantage. They alone were permitted into the fabled confines of the harem; they alone could observe the decadent lives of the sultry wives and slaves of wealthy pashas and beys. So they went in the hundreds, propelled by curiosity or pushed by their husbands, who were keen to know what these forbidden palaces concealed.

Before the mid-nineteenth century, visitors to this region usually travelled by horse or mule and camped or slept in rough inns, known as khans or caravanserai. Women had difficulties finding accommodation if they lacked contacts. In 1810, Hester Stanhope wisely sent two male members of her party ahead to Constantinople to arrange a place to stay. In 1842, solo traveller Ida Pfeiffer lodged at Mme Balbiani's, a clean but simple hotel, the arrangements for which she made before leaving her boat. If she hadn't been able to stay there, she wrote, she would have been "badly off."[1]

Travellers were also advised to hire a guide, called a dragoman. Dragomans could make or break a journey, and most women became quite fond of theirs. Margaret Fountaine, a world traveller and butterfly collector, began a passionate affair with her dragoman, Khalil Neimy, that lasted for twenty-seven years. Harriet Martineau may not have fallen in love, but she still heartily recommended hers, Alee Mustafa: "When I saw what their knowledge of languages was,—what their efficiency in daily business, their zeal in traveling, and their familiarity with the objects *en route* wherever we went . . . I felt that some of us might look very small in our vocations, in comparison." Baedeker's *Egypt* recommended drawing up a contract with these indispensable men and provided sample wording.[2]

"My friends must pardon me for describing my cares so minutely, but I only do so to warn all those who would wish to undertake a journey like mine, without being either very rich, very high-born, or very hardy, that they had much better remain at home."—Ida Pfeiffer[3]

Lady Mary Wortley Montagu in her Turkish finery complete with turban and dagger. W. Greatbatch, Montagu, vol. 1, frontispiece.

➤"The lady that seemed the most considerable among them, entreated me to sit by her, and would fain have undressed me for the bath. I excused myself with some difficulty. They being, however, all so earnest in persuading me, I was at last forced to open my shirt, and shew them my stays; which satisfied them very well; for, I saw, they believed I was locked up in that machine, and that it was not in my own power to open it, which contrivance they attributed to my husband."
—Lady Mary Montagu[4]

TURKEY

The first woman to reveal the secrets of the harem to the West was Lady Mary Wortley Montagu, whose travels took her to Turkey in 1717 with her husband, ambassador Edward Wortley Montagu. Her account, in the form of letters, was first circulated in 1725. Filled with scandalous tales of her visits to harems and baths in Adrianople (Edirne) and Constantinople, the letters were daring not only because they were the first believable descriptions of such places but also because they elaborated on the states of voluptuousness found therein. During one visit she witnessed a dance, the like of which she had never seen before: "The tunes so soft!—the motions so languishing!—accompanied with pauses and dying eyes! half-falling back, and then recovering themselves in so artful a manner, that I am very positive the coldest and most rigid prude upon earth could not have looked upon them without thinking of *something not to be spoken of.*"[5]

Her familiarity with harems led her to mock the many male travellers who criticized the cloistered state of Eastern women. "Turkish ladies," she wrote, "are perhaps more free than any ladies in the universe, and are the only women in the world that lead a life of uninterrupted pleasure exempt from cares."[6]

But Montagu did not squander all her hours in Turkey smoking narghilehs with idle houris. Having lost a brother to smallpox and having herself been

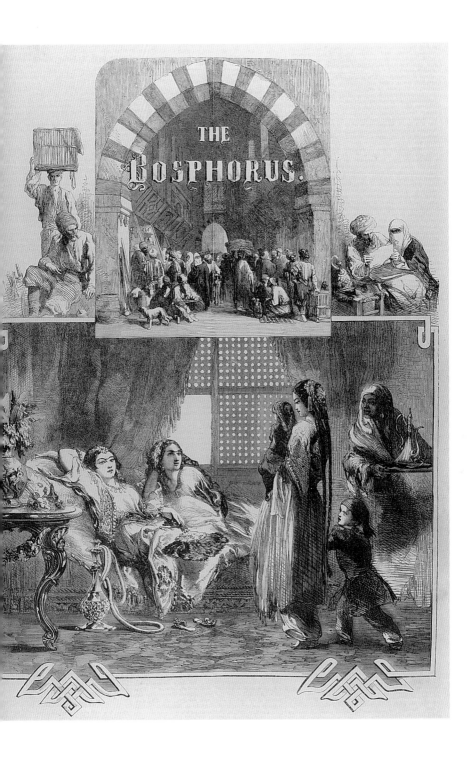

THE
BOSPHORUS.

Lady Redcliffe visiting the wounded at Scutari. The sedan chair in which Redcliffe rode was a common means of conveyance through Constantinople's busy, narrow streets.
ILN, 18 August 1855: 212.

scarred by it, she learned about inoculation from old women who carried it out every autumn. She had her children vaccinated and brought the practice to England.[7]

Lady Craven, who made her journey to Constantinople in 1785, decided that Montagu's letters were forgeries and could only have been written by a man, possibly Horace Walpole.★ She claimed that in Constantinople she was received by the ambassador to France and from her rooms at his mansion could spy on the sultan as he lounged about on his sofa.[8]

Generations of women travellers to the Middle East were influenced by Lady Montagu's *Letters* and expected to share her experiences and delight. The craze for things oriental swept through Europe in the 1700s, and with Napoleon's studies of Egypt (published in 1809), the writings of Chateaubriand and Lamartine and the paintings of Jean-Léon Gérôme and Delacroix, to name a few, orientalism became firmly established.

By the 1840s, harem visiting in Constantinople was getting out

---

★ Walpole of all people would have been a good candidate to have written Montagu's letters, having played the forgery game when he tried to pass off his novel *The Castle of Otranto* (1765) as a lost manuscript from the past.

Imagine walls blackened and cracked, wooden ceilings riddled with splits and coated with dust and spiders' webs, sofas ripped and greasy, portieres in shreds, traces of candle oil and grease everywhere. When I first entered one of these charming hideaways, I was shocked, but the ladies of the house didn't notice. They themselves are in keeping with the place. Mirrors being quite rare, the women deck themselves out in frippery whenever they can, the bizarre effect of which they couldn't possibly appreciate.

—Cristina di Belgiojoso[9]

Engraving, after A Visit (harem interior; Constantinople, 1860), by Henriette Browne. A professional artist, Browne visited Constantinople, Morocco, Egypt and Syria, and incorporated orientalist themes into her paintings.
Mettais, Tour du monde 8, 1863: 153.

of hand. When Lady Londonderry asked the British ambassador if he could get her into the sultan's harem, he turned her down flat, remarking that if he complied with every such request he'd be doing nothing else. She finally convinced Austria's ambassador to make the arrangements but had to settle for a harem lower down on the social scale.[10]

Some visitors to Constantinople were immediately enthralled; others, like Emmeline and Victoria Wortley, who visited in 1855 during the Crimean War, were critical. Victoria shared the opinion of her maid, who was "so disgusted with the atrocious state of the streets, that she wishes the Russians would come and take it tomorrow, if they only would make it decently clean!" Pragmatic Emily Beaufort, who arrived in 1860 after a long journey through Egypt and Palestine, thought that those coming directly from cold, damp England might be tricked "into fancying the real beauty of the place greater than it is."[11]

Cristina di Belgiojoso was intrigued enough with Turkey to make it her home for a few years. This powerhouse Italian patriot and princess, who had temporarily fled Austrian-ruled Lombardy when the embalmed body of her beloved secretary was found hidden in her villa, sailed with her daughter, Maria, and English maid, Mrs. Parker, into Constantinople in August 1849. By November 1850, she had bought a small farm overlooking the Bosphorus in a valley called Eiaq-Maq-Oglou. After a successful harvest of wheat and opium poppies, she turned the farm over to an Alsatian overseer, then left on a journey to Syria and Palestine. The resulting book, *Asie Mineure et Syrie (Oriental Harems and Scenery)* (1858), along with her articles in *Le Revue des deux mondes* (1855), revealed her thoughts on harem life and belly dancing, both of which left her cold; Jerusalem, which deeply affected her; and hashish, which produced few sensations except physical discomfort.[12]

Back at her farm eleven months later, Belgiojoso was appalled at its state of neglect and at how much money, which she was running short of, its restoration would take. To top it off, she learned that her assets in Italy had been confiscated. Then, in June 1853, a Lombard employee, who'd been having an affair with Mrs. Parker, stabbed Belgiojoso five times. She survived, nursing herself back to a semblance of health, but she was never the same; along with her energy, she had lost her youth and beauty. She returned to Europe.

SYRIA *and the* HOLY LAND

Constantinople was a jumping-off point for journeys to the Holy Land, the enduring goal of women pilgrims. In the nineteenth century, pilgrimage was the most acceptable excuse for travel, especially for those proposing to go on their own. The outspoken, aristocratic Lady Hester Stanhope needed no such reason. She wrote nothing of her extraordinary travels or legendary sojourn in the Levant, but because of her eccentric and flamboyant character, her fame was nonetheless assured.

After becoming estranged from her rich and volatile father, Stanhope lived with her uncle, Britain's prime minister William Pitt, from 1803 until his death in 1806. Witty, independent and eligible, she fit in well with Pitt's high-powered circle. She also spent part of 1805 as lady-in-waiting to the soon-to-be exiled Caroline, Princess of Wales. When Pitt died, her power was reduced, as were her means; parliament granted her an insubstantial annual income of £1200. Her grief at Pitt's passing was compounded by the deaths in 1809 of her half-brother Charles and of Sir John Moore, with whom she had fallen in love. Both died fighting in the war against Spain.[13]

In February 1810, Stanhope and her other half-brother, James, hitched a ride to Gibraltar on a frigate. She also brought her maid, Elizabeth Williams; a manservant; and her physician, Dr. Charles Meryon, whom she belittled mercilessly. Stanhope met and became the lover of Michael Bruce, a twenty-one-year-old on the

Hester Stanhope at Djoún. Meryon, vol. 2, frontispiece.

➤ "For hours, and hours, this wondrous white woman poured forth her speech, for the most part concerning sacred and profane mysteries; but every now and then, she would stay her lofty flight, and swoop down upon the world again; whenever this happened, I was interested in her conversation."
—Alexander Kinglake[14]

Grand Tour with his friend Lord Sligo. She took these new companions with her to Constantinople via Greece, where they briefly
met Byron.

When Stanhope, Bruce, Meryon and a new maid, Anne Fry,
sailed for Egypt in October 1811, their ship foundered off the coast
of Rhodes; no one died, but they lost their belongings. Having no
spare clothes, Stanhope and Fry donned Turkish men's attire. The
trip resumed; the party landed in Alexandria, then went on to
Cairo. Stanhope wore a spectacular brocade and gold-embroidered
turban, vest and pantaloons to meet ruler Mehemet Ali, but as he
apparently had never met a European woman before, her outfit did
not astound him.[15]

They departed for Palestine in May 1812, well equipped with
servants and bodyguards. Stanhope immediately established her
daring by riding unveiled into Damascus. There she met with a
sheikh of the Anazeh, the tribe controlling the desert routes, to plan
her expedition to Palmyra, the site of the ruined empire of Queen
Zenobia, where no European woman had been since Roman
times. In March 1813, Stanhope and Fry, dressed as Bedouin men,
began the arduous trip. Word sped along the desert grapevine;
everyone wanted to see this wealthy, defiant Englishwoman, and
her arrival was greeted with great celebration. To Stanhope it was
as though she had been accorded a queen's welcome.[16]

But the expedition set Stanhope back financially; hiring servants, guides, camels, tents and supplies, as well as paying the
sheikh for his protection, cost a fortune. She was fast going broke,
spending well beyond her income. Bruce and Stanhope's affair
cooled, so he left for England, promising her, but never sending,
half his yearly allowance. Back in Europe, he renounced their
friendship by insulting her, claiming she was unhinged.[17]

In an effort to salvage her precarious financial situation, she
resolved to find a reportedly buried hoard of money at Ascalon
and obtained permission to dig. She found no treasure, though the
party turned up artifacts, including a fine statue, which she had
destroyed lest anyone misinterpret her intentions. The excavation
put her further into debt.

She settled first at Mar Elias, then at Djoûn, a former
monastery in the Lebanon mountains northeast of Sidon, where
the household and its burdens swelled uncontrollably. Her guests

over the years included the English explorer James Silk Buckingham, who dedicated *Travels to Mesopotamia* to her; William Bankes, future MP for Cambridge, who slandered her; Alexander Kinglake, who wrote a strangely oblique portrait of her in *Eothen;* and Alphonse de Lamartine, who flattered her in *Voyage en Orient.*

Dr. Meryon left for England in 1817. Stanhope buried herself in astrology and fortune-telling, and her health, never perfect, declined. After civil war broke out, she asked Meryon to come back, but he had married and was reluctant to leave his wife, so he brought Mrs. Meryon with him. Their first efforts were stymied by an unnerving encounter with pirates. They tried again and finally succeeded in reaching Djoûn, where Mrs. Meryon and Stanhope put each other's back up.

Princess Caroline Amelia Elizabeth of Brunswick. From a painting by Thomas Lawrence, Bury, vol. 2, frontispiece.

By this time, Stanhope was living in poverty, yet she maintained some thirty servants and hangers-on. Then, the British government halted her pension on the grounds that she had unpaid debts in Egypt. She wrote letters of protest to Queen Victoria, Wellington and Palmerston, all to no effect. Back in England again, Meryon pleaded her case, also to no avail, then came out once more at her request. When he left for the final time, she had her house sealed up, and as far anyone could tell, lived for several months completely alone.[18] On 23 June 1839, this incredible iconoclast died.

Whereas Stanhope was eccentric, Princess Caroline made her mark by bravado and indiscretion. Living with her husband, the Prince of Wales, later George IV, only long enough to produce one miserable and unloved daughter, Caroline embroiled herself in scandalous political machinations, alleged adultery and globe-trotting. She was exiled in 1814 and used the opportunity to waste considerable sums of money on lush villas in Italy before heading for Constantinople. Rumour has it that when Stanhope heard of the princess's imminent arrival in Syria, she fled.[19] To mark her journey on horseback from Acre to Jerusalem, Caroline commissioned a

portrait, *The Entry of St. Caroline into Jerusalem*. She
also founded a religious order that carried her name.
Caroline eventually went back to Italy and then to
England, where the prince regent instituted proceed-
ings for divorce on the grounds of adultery (later
dropped) and where she was barred from attending
his coronation.

Stanhope's expedition to Palmyra broke barriers for many travellers who followed in her footsteps. The next woman on record
to visit the fabled ruins was Jane Digby el-Mezrab, the former
Lady Ellenborough. Digby never wrote a memoir, but she did
keep diaries, to which biographer Mary Lovell had access. From
them, Lovell was able to piece together the details of Digby's
amazing and imperfectly known life. It's hopeless to try to con-
dense her many love affairs; she was a passionate woman who
captured the heart of Bavarian king Ludwig I before he met Lola
Montez; rode into the Macedonian hills with rebel Palikares leader
Xristodolous Hadji-Petros; and finally settled into marriage with
Bedouin sheikh Medjuel el-Mezrab.

When Digby, accompanied by her French maid, Eugénie, first
arrived in Syria, she was still reeling from her discovery that
Eugénie had also been sleeping with Hadji-Petros. They landed in
Beirut and immediately made their way to Damascus, where she
began making arrangements to go to Palmyra. In June 1853, she

embarked on what she called "her greatest adventure."[20] The Anazeh caravan she travelled with was attacked, she filled the twenty-four hours allotted to her in Palmyra exploring the ruins, she commenced sleeping with Saleh, the caravan leader, and she met Medjuel.

She returned briefly to Greece but was back in Damascus a few months later and met Medjuel a second time. She told him she was thinking of buying a house in Damascus, and he asked her to marry him. Before replying, she went to Baghdad and had an affair with Sheikh el-Barak; when she returned, she agreed to marry Medjuel on the condition that he divorce his existing wife. After she made one more trip to Greece, Digby and Medjuel married and remained together until her death in 1881. She made frequent trips to Palmyra, became renowned for her Bedouin ways and her horsemanship, and was visited by many Middle East travellers, including Emily Beaufort, Isabel Burton, Lydie Paschkoff and Anne Blunt. Burton wrote of magical evenings spent on the roof of Digby's house, smoking in the company of the dashing exiled Algerian rebel leader Abd el-Kader.

In 1859, Emily Beaufort and her sister, R.E.B., travelled with Medjuel's caravan to Palmyra, where locals launched an impromptu auction for them. "In spite of the assurance that Frank women were never thus sold," Beaufort wrote, "they continued to bid us; and after shaking my head at some of their offers, one man enthusiastically rose to the sum of 10,000 piasters; but ... when told decidedly that he could not have me at any price, he turned away and said, 'I would have offered another thousand if her eyes had been black!'"[21]

Another visitor to Palmyra, Isabel Burton, lived in Damascus with her husband, celebrated explorer and British consul Richard Burton, from 1870 to 1871. Aside from plague, cholera, fleas, dust, famine, droughts and bandits, she found Damascus to be a tolerable place for a European woman. Her first introduction to the city was Demetri's, an inn that had drawn both praise

Emily Beaufort, here Lady Strangford.
Graphic, 26 May 1877: 496.

➤"My destination was Damascus, the dream of my childhood and girlhood. I am to live amongst the Bedouin Arab chiefs; I shall smell the desert air; I shall have tents, horses, weapons and be free."—Isabel Burton[22]

Isabel Burton in 1869. Photo by
P. Naumann, Burton 1898, facing p. 350.

🖎"I thought what a fine
thing the sheet and the veil
would be to some of our
European women."
—Isabel Burton[23]

and scorn. Of it she wrote, "It is a good house with a fine courtyard, which has orange and lemon trees, a fountain full of goldfish in it, and a covered gallery running round it." Other travellers hadn't been so kind; twenty years earlier Harriet Martineau had been furious to find no orange trees, no goldfish, no fine courtyard, and declared, "It is not right in travelers to romance about such houses as these, whether they be in the East or elsewhere: for future comers suffer by the complacency or indolence of the proprietor."[24]

Burton frequented the *hammans,* or baths, where she was warmly received. Her account would not inspire romantics: "I was rather shocked. They squat naked on the floor, and, despoiled of their dress and hair and make-up, are, most of them, truly hideous. Their skins are like parchment, and baggy; their heads as bald as billiard-balls. What little hair they have is dyed an orange red with henna. They look like the witches in *Macbeth,* or at least as if they had been called up from out of the lower regions . . . An average Englishwoman would look like an *houri* amongst them; and their customs were beastly, to use the mildest term." Still, the experience encouraged her to try the *hammans* in London and Paris, which she denounced as "puddles of dirty water."[25]

As the consul's wife, Burton was given escorts for her forays into the city and the countryside. She justified the expense by pointing out that women who went out alone were subjected to insults, and she recalled an incident in which a young lady who had travelled by diligence from Beirut to Damascus had been kissed "all the way up" by a Persian gentleman. "Poor little idiot! . . . She had the Persian arrested . . . If anybody had tried that sort of game on with me, I should have made an example of him myself, and taken the law in my own hands, whoever he was."[26]

Burton also described the unorthodox Duchesse de Persigny, the beautiful teller of racily unrepeatable tales whose behaviour did not set a good example for other women visitors. According to Burton, her prank at a mosque, when she refused to come down from the minaret, was especially audacious: "The Shaykh sent all kinds of emissaries and entreaties, to whom she replied, 'Dites au Shaykh que je suis la Duchesse de Persigny, que je me trouve fort bien ici, et que je ne descendrai que quand cela me plaira.' She did not please for three-quarters of an hour."[27] Guards hired to protect her begged the French consul to consider their reputations and not ask them to do such work.

By the time Russian journalist and traveller Lydie Paschkoff left for Palmyra in 1872, at least ten western women (including identified maids) had already been: in addition to those mentioned above, Dutch travellers Alexine and Harriet Tinne and their maid Flora travelled there in 1857. This didn't mean the trip had become a piece of cake, so Paschkoff planned accordingly. The previous custom of arranging for a Bedouin escort was no longer practised; travellers now paid Turkish soldiers for protection. Her group, which included her dragoman, Fadull, and two maids, grew with the addition of the Russian consul, a French photographer and their attendants.

Her equipment was so excessive that she needed thirty-three mules to carry bags, thirty-five camels for water, twenty donkeys for the camel drivers and twelve horses for the soldiers. As the women were unable to endure long treks, the caravan would start after lunch, and travel would be limited to six hours a day.

That Lydie Paschkoff had money is evident from the scale of her expedition. Just consider the meal she offered to local dignitaries:

> We had for dinner some Potel and Chabot conserves, good soup, lobsters, asparagus and game pies; roasted veal and chickens, and at the end a nice plum pudding, all washed down by an excellent Bourgogne and a decent Champagne, not including coffee, raki and liqueurs. The good pascha said to his aides-des-camp: "Is this a dream, messieurs? . . . [I]t's without doubt to the auspicious genies of these ruins that we owe this good windfall; we fear that these tents may also disappear from magic."[28]

Visiting sheikhs were so astonished by Paschkoff's clothes that

Lydie Paschkoff at Palmyra.

E. Ronjat, *Tour du monde* 33, 1872: 163.

they asked permission to inspect them. We would too if we saw her clambering about in embroidered blue satin slippers garnished with Paris-made lace.[29]

Whereas Paschkoff travelled in high style, Anne Blunt who visited Palmyra in 1878 with her husband, Wilfrid Scawen Blunt, was equipped only with necessities. Anne, the well-off daughter of Ada Byron Lovelace and granddaughter of Byron, first met Wilfrid in Italy in 1866. Then an aspiring poet and an attaché for the British government, Wilfrid was also broke, so marriage appealed to him, even though it might cramp his style as a womanizer. (It didn't.) They were married in June 1869; by August Anne was pregnant. Over the next seven years, as the couple travelled through North Africa and the Middle East, she became pregnant at least nine times, but only one child survived, the prematurely born Judith. Anne miscarried frequently; in Algeria, a fetus was buried in the dead of night.[30]

They were both smitten by the East; Anne—who knew of her husband's philandering—was probably grateful that Muslim countries temporarily halted his amorous activities. The pair arrived at Aleppo in November 1877, where they planned a circuit east to Baghdad, north along the Tigris, returning to Aleppo via Palmyra. The result of this trip, one of the goals of which was to improve their knowledge of Bedouin customs and Arabic, was Anne's *Bedouin Tribes of the Euphrates* (1879), the authorship of which she attributed to Wilfrid, and which he, in fact, heavily edited. Although travel through this area was still uncertain—made more so by unrest throughout the Ottoman Empire—and living conditions were rough, her account is straightforward and uncomplaining. They rode through snow and rain, then through choking, dry heat, and they shared filthy, cramped quarters with other travellers at lowly khans, camped in the tents they had specially made or were guests of consuls, governors and princes. In 1879 they made a second trip, through the Nejd desert and east to Baghdad and India.

Both the Burtons' and the Blunts' sojourns in Palestine coincided with the arrival of organized tour groups. In 1871, a year after the first Cook's tour to the Holy Land, Burton ran into a group at Beirut: "They swarmed like locusts over the town, in number about one hundred and eighty; and the natives said of them, 'These are not travellers; they are Cookii.'" The Blunts, on their return from the desert in 1878, happened across a rowdy, scantily dressed crowd at their Beirut hotel. Their first thought was that these rabble-rousers were on a Cook's jaunt and were shocked when told that they were high-class visitors who had come by yacht.[32]

For all the vaunted suppression of women in the Middle East, many European women found incredible independence, especially through opportunities to deal with men on an equal basis. Cultural differences aside, travellers often developed easygoing yet mutually respectful friendships with Arab men, many of whom were fluent in English or French. In contrast, Arab women remained no more than a curiosity, not only because of their sequestered existences, but also because of the language barriers.

> April 1878, Damascus: "I had to get ready to go to the tiresome harem. A harem is a thing to see, so people say, and here I had a golden opportunity."—Anne Blunt[31]

FOLLOWING PAGES:
"*Tourists Ascending the Great Pyramid*"(detail).
R. Caton Woodville, *ILN*, 7 May 1887: 530–31.

Egypt *Leave Your Crinoline in Cairo*

GEOGRAPHICALLY, EGYPT BELONGS TO AFRICA, but few travellers thought of it that way. It was simply Egypt, a country like no other. Some travellers came across the Sinai; the rest arrived by sea at Alexandria, ready to commence a two- to three-month tour. The drill, once the anchor dropped, was to fend off the touts that swarmed the boat, fight through customs, escape to a hotel, then express deep regret for having made the trip.

Alexandria's sights—the catacombs, Pompey's Pillar—were dismissed as third-rate, so most travellers immediately hired a dragoman and made their way by boat or mule to Cairo (before train service began in 1856). At Cairo, they became reconciled to the country and began looking forward to their tour up the Nile to Aswan or even farther to Nubia.

Before the completion of the Suez Canal in 1863, travellers bound for India via the Red Sea went from Alexandria to Cairo, then across to Suez, where boats for Madras, Ceylon or Bombay awaited them. One such traveller was Eliza Fay. At the end of July 1779, she and her husband sailed into Alexandria; a month later they were off to Cairo, fearful of the plague gripping the city. Their worries were justified; they both fell ill but soon recovered.

In Cairo, Fay wandered around in the heat, suffocating in a cloak and veil. Recent reports of mistreatment of Europeans crossing the desert terrified her. An escapee from an especially devastating raid did nothing to calm her when he cried out, "Oh Madam how unhappy you are in having come to this wretched place," leading to moans of "What shall we do with the lady?" Treachery was expected daily, so Fay hid in the house of an Italian doctor and his family and waited with them for several days in a state of alarm. "Imprisonment and massacre in every shape,

Shepheard's Hotel, Cairo. Initially established to serve customers who were passing through on their way to or from Suez, Shepheard's became the place to stay in Cairo. In 1884, the Sudan War was in full swing, and many battle plans were discussed on the hotel's veranda. Women were at ease in this hotel, but they could not go to see the female orchestra at the café chantant across the street.[1] ILN, 9 February 1884: 140–41.

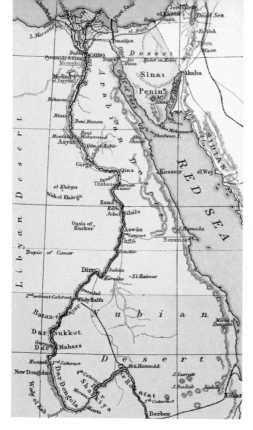

ABOVE: *Egypt and Nubia.*
The Handy Atlas, c. 1900.
BELOW: *At the railway*
station, Alexandria.
ILN, 25 April 1857: 378.

were the sole subjects of their conversation," she sighed.[2] Rumours abounded. They were to be sent as prisoners to Constantinople; their belongings were to be confiscated. Then suddenly they were given permission to depart. When they finally set across the burning sands, they felt great trepidation. Would they survive the three-day journey? We'll have to wait until India to find out.

Another who travelled through Egypt on her way to India and paused long enough to scrape together material for a book was Emma Roberts, who wrote *Notes of an Overland Journey through France and Egypt to Bombay* (1841). Conditions on the Cairo-Suez route had improved sufficiently by 1839 that Roberts could marvel that "ladies, having only three servants and a few donkey-drivers, required no other protection, though our beds, dressing-cases, and carpet-bags, to say nothing of the camels laden with trunks and portmanteaus a-head, must have been rather tempting to robbers." She appears to have been lucky; an 1844 report told of a European man on his way to Suez, who was stripped of absolutely everything and left, with hands tied behind his back, to find his own way.[3]

Travellers also trekked through the desert to go to or come from Palestine. They had to hire guides and protection, because the route was even more gruelling and dangerous than the one from Cairo to Suez. Of her Sinai crossing in 1847, Harriet Martineau wrote, "I would never say a word to encourage any woman to travel in the Desert," yet she claimed her health, which was almost always poor, flourished there.[4] She and her party alternatively rode camels, walked or were carried in palanquins, or litters. She must have looked a treat with her broad-brimmed sun hat, black-wire goggles and ear trumpet—for she was quite deaf.

Martineau wrote *Eastern Life, Present and Past* (1848), an earnest travelogue filled with observations of Eastern faith, customs, history and archaeology. Accompanied by three friends, she cruised up the Nile in a *dahabiya,* the standard means of travel. At this time, boats were often sunk before the trip commenced. Visitors were horrified to find out that the sinking was to kill bugs infesting the boats. The success of the process was too often short-lived, giving travellers a chance to scratch their way to Aswan. Martineau was proud that her boat was bug-free enough to skip the sinking.

On board, she and her friend, Mrs. Yates, occupied themselves by sewing and ironing, of all things. This was so diverting that Martineau recommended that a lady think of "putting up a pair of flat-irons among her baggage. If she can also starch, it will add much to her comfort."[5] On land, however, she redeemed herself by diligently recording everything.

ABOVE: *Harriet Martineau*. Alonzo Chappel, Duyckinck, vol. 2, facing p. 370. BACKGROUND: *Nile* dahabiya. Bayard Taylor, *Central Africa*, New York: G. P. Putnam, 1864, 85.

By the 1840s, Egypt was flooded with women eager to record their delight or disgust with the country. The long list of authors and their books included Georgiana Damer, *Diary of a Tour in Greece, Turkey, Egypt, and the Holy Land* (1841); Ida Von Gräfin Hahn-Hahn, *Orientalische Briefe* (c. 1845); and Isabella Romer, *A Pilgrimage to the Temples and Tombs of Egypt, Nubia, and Palestine* (1846). Romer boasted of stealing a statue from the ruins at Beni Hasan, provoking Martineau to censure her behaviour.[6]

A far more erudite visitor was Sophia Poole, author of *An Englishwoman in Egypt* (1844). Poole, sister of Edward Lane, the much-venerated Egyptian scholar, saw Egypt in the early 1840s with her brother's guidance. She mixed history, economics and statistics with her edited correspondence, hoping it would be

The governor of Esneh was keen to see "the novel, and to him incomprehensible sight of a *hareem belonging to nobody,* travelling in blissful liberty by itself on the Nile!"—Emily Beaufort[7]

more favourably received than a mere collection of chatty letters. All very admirable, said *Blackwood's* reviewer, but he wanted to get to the really interesting part of the book—"whither no male footstep can ever penetrate—the harems." She satisfied his curiosity with details of clothing, jewellery, cosmetics and topics of conversation. But she also noted her triumph of visiting the Al Azhar mosque, to which Christians, especially ladies, had been forbidden entrance.[8]

Emily Beaufort and her sister chose to go to Egypt in 1858, "believing that we should find there an endless store of deeply interesting subjects for thought and study, unfatiguing travelling, and no society; our hopes of the two former were more than realised, but solitude is difficult to obtain on the now fashionable and crowded Nile."[9] How she could have described their tour as "unfatiguing" is a mystery. While docked at Edfu on their return from Nubia, fire consumed their *dahabiya* and all of their possessions.

For the next two weeks, the sisters were at the mercy of sympathetic European women—of whom there were all too few—to supply them with necessities. Beaufort remarked bitterly that "we found our country*men* far more generous and thoughtful for us than our country*women*."★[10] They limped back to Cairo and replaced their luggage with much difficulty and expense, then faced the decision of whether to sue the boatman. Their quandary was resolved when the boatman sued them—for libel. The consul advised them to get out of the country as fast as they could.

Excitement did not desert the Beauforts when they sailed from Alexandria. They took a house in the mountains near Beirut, where they were caught in the middle of the 1859 conflict between the Druze and the Christians. They fled, then later heard that "one of us had been murdered in the battle, and that the other had escaped, with the maid, into the depths of the valley, where it was confidently expected, both would be immediately shot or starved to death!"[11] They were set upon by bandits just outside Damascus, at the beginning of their trek to Jerusalem; tumbled, with horse, off a steep slope while descending Mount Hermon; were robbed, but recovered their bags, near the Dead Sea; and their

★ Beaufort became Lady Strangford, renowned for her charitable works.

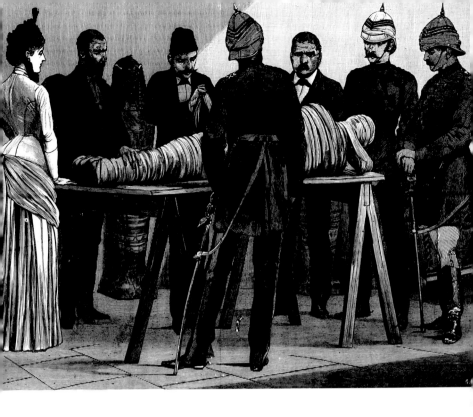

maid fell off her horse and was knocked unconscious. They then continued north to further mishap in Turkey and Greece.

Although harem visits were all the rage in Egypt as in Constantinople, the pyramids exerted a stronger pull. No one left Cairo without making the trip to Giza. Of the many women who wrote of climbing the pyramids—Pfeiffer, Beaufort, Martineau—all warned away any lady who was "subject to dizziness," "seized with panic" or "not entirely sure of her own nerves and self-control."[12]

Sophia Poole rang a different sort of alarm; during her trip to the pyramids, the party met up with a couple of young Bedouin, who had earlier espied a very pretty American and wanted to see more such beauties. Since Poole and her female companions were veiled, their hopes were dashed. The young men admitted they had been tempted to abduct the American, prompting Poole to remark, "Tis well . . . that these lawless Arabs are kept under a degree of subjection by the present government."[13]

"Unwrapping Ancient Mummies in the Boulak Museum of Cairo." Mummies were regularly unveiled for the benefit of scholars and tourists alike, often in hotels as part of a day's sightseeing activities. ILN, 31 July 1886: 125.

FOLLOWING PAGES:
"Starting for the Pyramids: A Sketch at Cairo." I.W. Bromley, ILN, 3 October 1874: 316–17.

Ascension de Pyramide N°8

It's been three days since I made the trip, or rather, the voyage, I am still broken, I have pains in my arms, in my legs, and I can't make a move without suffering, it's in pain that I can take the pen up to recount to you our expedition, because that's what it truly was.—Olympe d'Audouard[14]

In 1864, when Olympe d'Audouard rode to the pyramids, it was still a major undertaking. A French writer and advocate of women's rights, Audouard had already travelled to Algeria, Morocco, Germany, Russia, Turkey and Palestine. Her stay in Egypt was enlivened by her suspicions that the Egyptian viceroy considered her a spy and had her under surveillance. She wrote of this and other experiences in her book *Les Mystères de l'Égypte dévoilés* (1866).

Her companions for the expedition were an old Englishman, his wife and two Parisian men. They had arranged to meet at dawn in the hotel lobby, but because Audouard chose to wear unfamiliar men's clothing, which took her awhile to figure out, and being a Parisienne unaccustomed to getting up before noon, she was late.

The Englishwoman was shocked at the sight of Audouard in trousers and refused to believe that her own crinolines would be a nuisance. The first test came with the mules; the Englishwoman, riding sidesaddle, threatened to fall off at intervals, yet screamed when her muleteer tried to keep her upright. Audouard didn't fare much better astride; the saddle battered her backside and ground into her abdomen, but she at least stayed on. When they reached the pyramids and began their climb, the Englishwoman refused to go up, conceding that Audouard had been right.

A good description of the climb was given by Emily Beaufort:

> The only right way to get through the ordeal is to be quietly passive in the hands of the three Arabs apportioned to each visitor . . . [T]hey know best how to tie up your garments so that they shall not impede your progress, and how to lift you with least exertion or disagreeability to yourself, and the sole piece of advice I give to my countrywomen is, to *let* them lift you, and—to leave your crinoline in Cairo.[15]

"Ascension de Pyramide, No. 8." Photo by Abdullah Frères, c. 1886–89.

Tourists in front of the Sphinx, c. 1900.

One couldn't escape reminders that scores of others had already made the climb. Among the scrawled names marring the summit was that of the "Swedish nightingale," Jenny Lind. "Fie on her!" wrote Victoria Wortley.[17]

What goes up must come down; Ida Pfeiffer described her descent:

Most people find this even more difficult than the ascent; but with me the contrary was the case. I never grow giddy, and so I advanced in the following manner, without the aid of the Arabs. On the smaller blocks I sprang from one to the other; when a stone of three or four feet in height was to be encountered, I let myself glide gently down; and I accomplished my descent with so much grace and agility, that I reached the base of the pyramid long before my servant. Even the Arabs expressed their pleasure at my fearlessness on this dangerous passage.[18]

~⁓ "My only outward memorial of this day is a small photograph . . . It represents the learned professor and his homely wife, with the awful background of Pyramid and Sphinx."
—Mrs. R. L. Bensly[16]

Almost everyone admired the pyramids; however, Florence Nightingale, who was in Egypt in 1850, had no scruples about denouncing them. She supposed that her unwillingness to faint in pleasure over them would mean that she would forever be an outcast, the result of being a "victim to truth." Florence and Rosamond Hill, who made a side trip to Egypt and the pyramids on their way to Australia in the early 1870s, dismissed them with a terse sentence: "A glimpse of Cairo, an ascent of the great pyramid, and a visit to Memphis are now events too common for us to venture on their description."[19]

"Levinge Bag." The virtues of this sleeping device, invented by Richard Levinge and designed to keep mosquitoes and other bugs at bay, were extolled by Florence Nightingale, in her diary of her Egyptian travels.

Nudity among Egyptians was frequently referred to by women travellers; Audouard bluntly stated that her guides to the pyramids stripped down to their birthday suits at the slightest excuse. Others described states of undress more coyly, but it's doubtful that anyone but Audouard would have dared write about a deflowering. Audouard, who attended a Coptic wedding, realized the customs were rather different from what she expected, so when asked if she'd like to stay for the post-marriage rites, she readily agreed and watched with a mixture of horror and fascination as the husband entered the bridal chamber and, in the presence of a score of women, including herself and her maid, ceremoniously deprived his new wife of her virginity. A white handkerchief showing the proof that the ritual had been successful was shown to others waiting outside the room.[20]

Lucie Duff Gordon, who lived in Luxor from 1862 until 1869 in an effort to ameliorate the consumption eating away at her lungs, was also frank in her descriptions. She was London-born, well-educated and accustomed to the lively conversation of a close-knit literary circle that consisted of Tennyson, Dickens and Thackeray.

Before settling in Egypt, she had first tried South Africa, sailing there with her maid, Sally Naldrett, and a goat. During a series of

Lucie Duff Gordon. Dronsart, 261.

Elephantine Island · Jan 27th 1868

Sketch of Marianne North painting on Elephantine Island in Egypt. R. Phené Spiers, North 1893, facing p. 133. storms en route, she had herself lashed to a support on the deck of the *St. Lawrence* to better enjoy the tempestuous conditions. She returned to England a year later, then travelled to Egypt the following winter, again with Sally. Her first reaction upon arrival in Alexandria was dismay, mirroring other travellers' responses. But in Cairo, she had the tremendous luck of finding Omar, a dragoman who was to stay with her for all her sojourns in Egypt, and she delighted in making arrangements for a *dahabiya* to take her to Luxor.

Duff Gordon's years in Egypt were recorded in letters to her family. Not initially meant for publication, they reveal a traveller with a sense of humour and a tolerance not at all common at the time. She openly expressed her admiration of the young native women in a letter to her husband: "If I can get hold of a handsome fellahah here, I'll get her photographed to show you in Europe what a woman's breast can be, for I never knew it before I came here—it is the most beautiful thing in the world. The dancing-girl I saw moved her breasts by some extraordinary muscular effort, first one and then the other; they were just like pomegranates and gloriously independent of stays or any support."[21]

She became the confidante of many Egyptians and involved herself in local issues, dispensed medicine and advice, and received European visitors, including Edward Lear, Katherine Petherick and Marianne North. Her equanimity rarely faltered, but she could not forgive Sally for suddenly producing a child fathered by Omar. (Omar, however, she considered foolish but not at fault.)[22]

In the end, not even the steady Luxor heat could save her; she died in July 1869. Her Egypt letters, published in 1865 and 1875, are a valuable record of the rises and dips of tourism along the Nile, the improvements to transportation (including the introduction of steamboats and the building of the Suez Canal), of the state of Egyptian politics and economics, and the customs and attitudes of Egyptians. She also gave unabashed reviews of other travellers' books. She praised her cousin Harriet Martineau's book *Eastern Life* for its descriptions of scenery but criticized Martineau's narrow and paternalistic view as revealed in such statements as "We treated them as children, and this answered perfectly well."[23]

Martineau's attitude could have been worse; many travellers, not always men, gave in to violence. Ida Pfeiffer, who would later prove an unflappable and equitable traveller under trying circumstances, felt driven to whip a muleteer. She explained why she mentioned the incident in her *Visit to the Holy Land, Egypt, and Italy* (1852): "I wish merely to give future travellers a hint as to the best method of dealing with these people. Their respect can only be secured by the display of a firm will; and I am sure that in my case they were the more intimidated as they had never expected to find so much determination in a woman."[24]

Egypt became, according to Emily Beaufort, "fashionable and crowded"; in other words, old hat to those seeking new experiences. However, continuing on meant crossing the inhospitable Libyan Desert or sailing up the Nile into Nubia. The desert route apparently lacked appeal; I have found no trace of women attempting such a journey. Those who went south usually turned back at Aswan, though a number did make it to Abu Simbel and even Wadi Halfa, near the second cataract. Of the land beyond, all that was known was that it was dangerous, festering with deadly diseases and inhabited by formidable and unclothed Africans. And no matter how you got there, it was no place for a lady.

Africa *No Place for a Lady?*

BEFORE EMILY BEAUFORT RELUCTANTLY turned back to Cairo, having made it as far south as the second cataract of the Nile, she carved her name into a rock that held "a mighty company of names," as proof that she, too, had made the incredible journey to Africa's borders.[1] By 1859, the year of her visit, few European women had got even that far; two years later, that was all to change. From 1861 to 1864, Nubia attracted four of the most important women travellers to Africa: Katherine Petherick, Florence Baker, and Alexine and Harriet Tinne.

CENTRAL AFRICA

Travels in Central Africa (1869) by Katherine and John Petherick described the couple's experiences in the Sudan during John Petherick's troubled tenure as British consul. Written mostly to exonerate him from accusations of slave trading and incompetence, the book is packed with thrilling details of danger and discovery. This voyage was Katherine's first to Africa and her husband's second.

By the time the Pethericks arrived in Khartoum in October 1861, Captains John Speke and James Grant had already embarked on their great exploration of the Nile. The Tinnes, daughter, mother and aunt, weren't to arrive until April of the following year. Samuel Baker and his companion and future wife, Florence, had started for Abyssinia (Ethiopia) in May 1861 and would eventually come to Khartoum in June 1862.

Travelling from Cairo to Khartoum by *dahabiya* and camel, the Pethericks endured scorching heat, a destructive thunderstorm and a plague of scorpions. Poignant reminders of the risks were the grave of Mary Walton, who had died earlier that year, and farther on, near the village of Abu Hamid, that of Andrew Melly, a Swiss-born Englishman who had died of fever ten years earlier, leaving his wife, two sons and daughter to fend for themselves.

Florence Baker. From *The Nile Tributaries of Abyssinia*, 1868, reprinted in *Harper's Weekly*, 28 June 1873: 561.

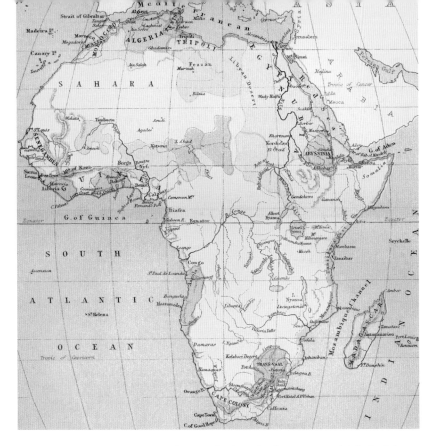

Africa. Philips' Handy Atlas, c. 1897.

Katherine had packed a piano, which had been manufactured in two parts for easy transport, but otherwise she was practical. To ride a camel like everyone else, she wore "yellow Turkish boots, very loose and uncomfortable; full Turkish trousers, but over them a brown holland skirt or petticoat, and a white flannel jacket with capacious pockets." She hid her mirror to spare herself the misery of seeing how frightful she looked.[2]

On their arrival at Khartoum, they began preparing, as previously agreed, to take relief to the southern station of Gondokoro for Speke and Grant. Advance boats were dispatched, but for the Pethericks themselves, setting off was easier said than done. Supplies had to be organized, then the wind turned against them and the Nile rose to its highest level in years. They finally left on 20 March 1862, only to collide with another boat. Storms flooded the cabins, and the boats developed continuous leaks.

En route, they were dismayed to encounter one of their boats on its way back, filled with slaves. They freed the slaves before letting the boat proceed, then continued on, unaware that this action would turn both Arab and European traders against them and would also lead to future accusations that John had become involved in the slave trade.

They had more immediate things to worry about. It was cold and wet, mosquitoes ruled supreme and many of the party succumbed to fever. By July 1862, with the hot season setting in, Katherine weakened from ague and dysentery. She continued to write unruffled entries in her journal; in one she described her outfit: "A short thick linsey petticoat, leather gaiters, strong boots, cloth jacket, leather gloves, and straw hat ... round my waist was buckled a five-barrelled revolver pistol secured in a small pouch." The friend who had given her this pistol had written that "it seems strange to offer a lady so deadly a weapon, but you are going to travel thousands of miles through country where even the buttons on your dress will appear a mine of wealth to its savage inhabitants. That you may never be called upon to use it is [my] sincere wish."[3]

John and Katherine Petherick. Petherick 1869, vol. 1, frontispiece.

A month later John Petherick took over the account; it is our first awareness of just how sick Katherine had become. Shortly after, their death by drowning was reported in the London newspapers, something they weren't aware of until almost a year later. They were by no means dead, but they came close as wave after wave of fever hit them.

By 15 February 1863, when they reached Gondokoro, four months after their appointed meeting date with Speke and Grant, there was no sign of the explorers. The Pethericks undertook a brief survey; while they were gone, Samuel and Florence Baker arrived at the trading station, as did Speke and Grant. When the Pethericks returned soon after, Speke, miffed at the consul's tardiness, turned down their supplies and accepted Samuel Baker's instead. Once back in England, Speke accused Petherick of neglect of duty and lobbied to get the consulate abolished.

For the next four months until their return to Khartoum, the Pethericks fought against typhus and malaria. When they finally

made the arduous journey back down the Nile to Cairo, Katherine, who had been so full of spirit on the way out, wanted to lie down and die. But she made it to Aswan, where she regained her health. Back in Cairo, they heard of Speke's demise; he had accidentally shot himself with a hunting rifle.

In dispatches to London during his 1861–64 expeditions to Abyssinia and the Albert Nyanza (Lake Albert), forty-year-old explorer and widower Samuel Baker made no mention of his twenty-year-old travelling companion, Florence Barbara Maria Finnian (von Sass). He had reason to be discreet; not only were they not married, though they were travelling as husband and wife, but he had bought her at a slave market in the Balkan town of Widden (Vidin) more than two years earlier and no one in his family knew of her existence. Her family (Hungarians from Transylvania, now part of Romania) had been massacred in 1848; she had somehow survived and had ended up on the auction block.[5]

Samuel had originally wanted to search for the source of the White Nile but was thwarted by the Royal Geographical Society's support of Speke and Grant. Instead, the couple explored the tributaries of the Blue Nile. After an extremely difficult year-long journey, during which both suffered terribly from illness and from conflict with Abyssinians, they made their way to Khartoum in

A. DEN.

Koch & Soligny sc

If it be a sin to covet honour, Mr. Baker must be one of the most offending souls alive. Other reasons for the perilous enterprise he undertook there appears to have been none, and there was one very strong reason why he should have avoided it—he was married, and a wife would seem at the first blush likely to be rather an encumbrance than a help to the adventurous traveller through unknown regions, through hordes of barbarians, through scenes of sickness and toil and danger and death . . . But as the flower safety is often plucked from the nettle danger, and as what seemed weakness is suddenly transformed into strength, so Mrs. Baker became an assistance instead of a drawback.[6]

Samuel and Florence Baker. Florence's African outfits were described as masculine by Harriet Tinne, but in engravings, her slightly raised skirt and boots seem to be her only concession to adventure.

A. de Neuville, *Tour du monde* 15, 1867: 9.

A welcome-back ceremony.
Tour du monde *adapted*
this illustration from
Baker's The Albert
N'yanza *for its excerpt,*
exaggerating the event in
all respects. Florence is
sorely out of place with her
crinolined skirt and fan.
A. de Neuville, *Tour du monde* 15,
1867: 37.

mid-June 1862. When Samuel met Speke and Grant at Gondokoro, they told him of a potential alternative source, the lake that came to be called the Albert Nyanza.[7]

This White Nile expedition was, if anything, even more spectacular than the Abyssinian venture. Now the Bakers had run-ins not only with Africans but also with slave traders, who saw them as a threat to their lucrative business. The sicknesses the couple had suffered earlier were just a warm-up; Florence came so close to death that Samuel ordered her grave to be dug.[8]

The expedition reached its goal in March 1864; in November, they faced the difficult journey back. At Gondokoro, where they hoped provisions would be waiting, they found nothing and continued to Khartoum in a boat that had carried victims of the plague.[9] The couple made their way back to Cairo, then London.

Throughout their African journeys, Florence had been introduced to other travellers as Mrs. Baker, and by the time they returned to England in late 1865, Samuel had decided to marry her—the ceremony was kept a secret—enabling him to formally acknowledge her in his books *The Albert N'yanza* (1866) and *The Nile Tributaries of Abyssinia* (1867).

They were feted by the Royal Geographical Society, Samuel was knighted, and Sir and Lady Baker returned to Central Africa early in 1870 and remained there until mid-1873, commissioned by Khedive Ismail to help halt the slave trade. This was their last trip to Africa; Florence settled comfortably into life in England, while Samuel dreamed of a return he was never to make.

The African adventures of Alexine (aka Alexandrine) Tinne and her mother, Harriet Tinne, are the stuff of legend. These two Dutch women—the daughter twenty-six years old, the mother, sixty-three—set off in 1862 to explore the Nile and eventually made their way to Gondokoro. Accompanied by Adriana Van Capellen, Harriet's forty-eight-year-old sister, an intrepid woman in her own right, they met with the disease and duplicity that greeted all explorers to the region. The women were marvelled at for their courage, they were accused of turning African exploration into a weekend jaunt and they were envied for the incredible wealth that enabled them to outfit their expedition well beyond the means of other explorers.

What is known of their adventures comes partly from Harriet's surviving diary entries and correspondence and partly from other travellers, especially the Pethericks. The Bakers shared the Nile with them but didn't meet them. A very readable account, *Travels of Alexine* by Penelope Gladstone, was published in 1970.

Alexine was the heiress of her father's immense sugar fortune. After his death in 1845, mother and daughter, who were veteran travellers, continued to wander, first around Europe, then to Egypt, where they made two cruises up the Nile, and then to the Holy Land, making the difficult journey to Palmyra. Early in 1862, they finalized their plans to again sail up the Nile to the interior of Africa.

They left Cairo in January 1862 in three *dahabiyat*. Their party consisted of the two of them and Van Capellen; their Egyptian cook, Halib, who had been with them since 1857; and janissary Osman Aga, who had been with them on their Egyptian visits since 1856. They also were accompanied by two Egyptian domestics, several Dutch servants, a number of guards, and Flora and Anna, the Tinnes' European maids. They brought a horse, a donkey, five dogs and heaps of baggage, including camera equipment and food for a year. At Korosko, about mid-point, they left the boats and continued overland with 102 camels and numerous donkeys to carry their gear. They reached Khartoum in April, where they were faced with their first desertions; the Dutch male servants returned north.

Alexine Tinne (left) and
Harriet Tinne.
Émile Bayard, *Tour du monde 22,*
1870–71: 293 and 292.

They obtained a *dahabiya* and a provisions boat for the next stage up the White Nile, with Khartoum's only steamer (which they hired for their exclusive use) to pull them partway. After much difficulty, they managed to get to the slave-trading station of Jebel Dinka. There they remained while Harriet returned briefly to Khartoum to take care of repairs and purchase more supplies. Halib went with her, because he required medical treatment. Her stay at Khartoum coincided with the Bakers, but it's just as well they didn't meet: the Tinnes' commandeering of the steamer had put a kink in Samuel's plans, and he was annoyed.[10]

When Harriet returned, the party continued south through the Sudd, a section of the river often made impassable by thick vegetation. Illness struck Alexine and some of the crew. Then, as they neared Gondokoro, Osman Aga died trying to prevent an accident with one of the *dahabiyat*.[11] This tragedy was the beginning of a series of disasters.

They arrived at Gondokoro on 30 September 1862; by the end of October, Van Capellen and some of the Egyptians had had enough. They returned to Khartoum, passing the Bakers, who were just starting out. Samuel would later write of how he had fired a greeting salute and how they had waved handkerchiefs at

each other. He added that he had little guessed what was in store for them.[12]

The Bahr al-Ghazal.
E. Tournois, after an engraving from
Plantæ Tinneanæ, Tour du monde 22,
1870–71: 292.

Alexine organized a second expedition, south to Lake No, then west to the Bahr al-Ghazal. They left on 5 February 1863, this time with the German scientists Hermann Steudner (who was to die shortly after) and Baron von Heuglin, and the Dutchman Baron d'Ablaing. Van Capellen remained in Khartoum.[13]

A few days later, Samuel Baker wrote to John Petherick, "The Dutch ladies with the steamer have gone to the Bahar-al-Ghazal, with the intention of reaching Mundo and going to the Equator. They have a large force with them. There should be a public house built on the Equator, where travellers could stop for a glass of beer: it is becoming a fashionable tour."[14] One of the irritating things about the Tinnes was their money. Baker accused them of driving up prices; whether this criticism was justified or whether he was just jealous is a matter for debate.

Speke and Grant had made their way back to Khartoum; there they met Van Capellen and advised her that her sister and niece were exposing themselves to untold dangers. They were right; by the time the expedition returned to Khartoum on 29 March 1864, they had been cheated, ambushed, starved and wrongly accused of trading in slaves, and illness had thinned their ranks cruelly. But in the meantime, they had successfully reached the Bahr al-Ghazal and met up with the Pethericks, who helped them restock their dwindling supplies. Between the Tinnes and Heuglin, the group had well over three hundred porters, as well as servants, guards and hangers-on.[15]

The party passed the village of Wau and continued for a few days to a small trading station, where they were obliged to halt to wait out approaching rains. Alexine went ahead to search for a suitable site to set up camp, and while she was away Harriet, who had been the healthiest of all, fell ill and died on 22 July. Her daughter was devastated and decided to return to Khartoum, though that decision meant renouncing all she had worked towards. But with the worsening weather, even giving up took time, and a month later, while they were still at the camp, Flora died. She was sixty and had been with the family for many years.[16]

Back in Khartoum, Van Capellen was worried; she had not heard from the expedition for some time, so she arranged to send supplies. The relief group met with Tinne—and her now-450-strong entourage—as she reached Wau in January 1864. Then, on 22 January, Anna died.[17]

Van Capellen, who had also been ill, managed to live until her niece's return. Katherine Petherick, who had nothing but admiration for Van Capellen, had written a few months earlier: "I am uneasy about dear Miss Von Capellan [sic]: this is no place for her; she is in my opinion a greater heroine than any woman I ever knew, her sacrifice is self, her long and solitary residence in Khartoum, without kindred, waiting only the return of those so dear to her."[18]

Alexine and the four coffins bearing her mother, aunt, Flora and Anna left for Cairo in July 1864. There isn't enough room to discuss the details of her subsequent stay in Cairo, her Mediterranean cruise and her purchase of the yacht *Meeuw*, so we'll jump to her move to Algiers in 1867 and her expedition into the Sahara.

NORTH AFRICA

Accompanied by a crew of several dozen, including the Dutch crew from her yacht and their wives; Abdullah, her servant from Cairo; and camels, horses and their drivers, Alexine Tinne left Algiers early in 1868 and struck south to the oasis of Touggourt. Bad weather and petty complaints from the sailors cut the expedition short. After a respite in Malta, she moved to Tripoli, then launched a new expedition to cross the Sahara on 30 January 1869. This caravan, also a large one, started more auspiciously; taking only two Dutch sailors may have helped. By March, they had travelled about eight hundred kilometres and had reached the town of Murzuq. There Tinne fell seriously ill and was forced to stop. When she recovered, the caravan resumed its way; two weeks later, on 1 August 1869, she was dead from a gunshot wound.[19]

Accounts of Tinne's murder were muddled and contradictory, but her death probably resulted from an argument between members of her caravan and those of another. It appears that as she stepped in to intercede, one of her sailors was stabbed and her

Alexine Tinne and her household at Algiers.
Émile Bayard, Tour du monde 22, 1870–71: 301.

hand was sliced off, then bullets started flying, and she and the remaining sailor were shot. Her caravan was plundered, and the survivors straggled back to tell their confused and tragic story.[20]

Up to that point, Libya had attracted few women travellers. The earliest that I can find was the so-called Miss Tully, described as the sister of the consul to Tripoli, Richard Tully. She was credited with writing *Narrative of a Ten Years' Residence at Tripoli in Africa* (1816). Although the preface compares her to Lady Montagu, the account is, unlike Montagu's writings, distant and probably apocryphal. Comments on architecture, the dress and habits of the royal family, coffee houses, the climate, plague, famine, harems, the consul's good standing, fill the pages, but there is little to tell us how she actually lived. She apparently stayed in Tripoli from 1783 until 1793, when civil strife drove her family out of Africa. Miss Tully may have been a fictional device, created by an anonymous writer.

In direct contrast to Libya, the Maghreb—Tunisia, Algeria and Morocco—was fertile and accessible and had been coveted by Phoenicians and Romans. Yet vast, uninhabitable areas, like the *bled* of southern Morocco, kept colonization limited to the coastal regions. By 1844, France controlled large stretches of valuable land and encouraged French families to settle in the Maghreb. Spain and England also had limited interests in the area, yet women travellers did not flock to the region.

Lady Montagu is the first woman traveller I've found to have written of North Africa. She visited Tunis in July 1718 and chatted with the women of Carthage but had little to report that wasn't insulting. Princess Caroline sailed to Tunis in April 1816, excited by the idea of freeing enslaved Christians. She was enchanted with the place and managed to picnic in Carthage before being ordered to leave by Lord Exmouth, who was on a slave-freeing mission himself.[21]

Elizabeth Marsh was sailing from Gibraltar to England in 1756, when her ship was boarded by Barbary pirates. She and her fellow passengers, including one James Crisp—whom she was obliged to identify as her husband, for her safety's sake—were taken to the Moroccan town of Salé and then transported by mule to the town of Morocco (Marrakech), where they were held prisoner. Marsh was much afflicted by her captivity; the rough travel and living conditions, her state of suspense at her future and her anguish at being

kept from her family rendered her unable to appreciate the uniqueness of her experience. When she was
finally freed some months later, she married Mr.
Crisp and wrote a diary of her trials.[22]

*"English Ladies Visiting a
Moor's House."* J. B. Burgess, *ILN*,
20 February 1875: 173.

Accounts by Frenchwomen of their travels in North
Africa are not as common as one would expect, given France's
involvement in the area. Aurélie Picard, who lived in Algeria from
1871 until her death in 1933, did not leave an account either, but
her story captured the imaginations of at least three biographers.
Not so much a traveller as an adventuress, she was born into a
lower-middle-class French family and dreamed of becoming rich
someday. When she caught the eye of a corpulent yet exotic and
wealthy Algerian sheikh, Sidi Ahmad al-Tijani, in Bordeaux, she
got her chance. They married in 1871, in spite of opposition from
family and governments, and she moved to Algeria with him, first
staying in relative luxury in Algiers, then in the forbidding isolation of his mud-walled village, Aïn Madhi. Picard lost no time
taking charge; the sheikh's two wives were sent packing,★ and she

---

★ Picard discovered a third one tucked away when this wife produced a son, Ali, seven
years later. She personally escorted the woman out of town, then raised Ali as her stepson.[23]

introduced French food and furniture. She learned Arabic and the intricacies of her husband's religious brotherhood, the Sufi order of the Tijaniya, and took over the household finances.[25]

In 1883, with a grant from the government, Picard hired hundreds of skilled artisans to build her a house at what became the oasis village of Qurdan (Kourdane). She also had a house in Algiers, where she installed her mother. Not all was paradise; the wealth she was amassing led to suspicions that she was in the pay of French intelligence, and her husband died in April 1897. She then married his brother, a mutually repugnant but financially advantageous move. When he passed away in 1911, she moved to Algiers and nursed her dying mother and her stepson, who had cancer. After their deaths, she moved back to France briefly. Unable to adjust to the cold and now unfamiliar country, she returned to Algeria.[26]

Whereas Picard thrived in Algeria, Swiss-born writer Isabelle Eberhardt slowly disintegrated there. The life of the enigmatic and disturbed Eberhardt has been analyzed from a number of angles. Her sporadic transformation into an Algerian man, Si Mahmoud, has especially intrigued scholars of orientalism and sexuality. Raised speaking Russian and French, she also became fluent in Arabic and came to consider herself Muslim.[27] She had ordinarily worn boy's clothing at her home in Geneva and kept her hair short.

Eberhardt first went to Algeria in May 1897, with her frail, fifty-seven-year-old mother, Mme Nathalie de Moerder, who converted to Islam and died later that year. From then on, Eberhardt restlessly and passionately travelled between Algeria and France, often in the guise of a man, whether Si Mahmoud or a European.★ Biographers are certain that the general acceptance by Algerians of Isabelle as Si Mahmoud was politeness rather than gullibility.[28]

In the summer of 1900, she met Slimène Ehnni, a twenty-four-year-old spahi officer (they eventually

> ✎ "Right now, I long . . . to sleep in the chilly silence of the night below stars that drop from great heights, with the sky's infinite expanse for a roof and the warm earth for a bed, in the knowledge that no one pines for me *anywhere on earth,* that there is no place where I am being missed or expected. To know that is to be free and unencumbered, a nomad in the great desert of life where I shall never be anything but an outsider."
> —Isabelle Eberhardt[24]

★ Eberhardt called herself Pierre Mouchet on her return to Marseille in 1901.[29]

married), and in November she was initiated into the Qadryas brotherhood, a Sufi order. She had her hair shaved close to the skull, dressed in Arab robes and lived rough. Perpetually short of cash, she spent little of what she did have on food, preferring instead the oblivion of kif and absinthe. Naturally slim, she became dangerously thin.[30]

French officials harboured suspicions that she was spying on them; others thought she was "neurotic and unhinged." Of her presence in the Saharan town of El Oued, Arab Bureau official Captain Gaston Cauvet wrote that she was likely there "principally to satisfy unhindered her dissolute tastes and her penchant for natives in a place where there are few Europeans."[31]

An attempt was made on her life at Behima in February 1901. After she recovered from the attack, she was expelled and returned to Marseille. Three months later, she was recalled to testify against the would-be assassin. She realized that she would have to wear European clothing for her appearance at court, but as she wrote to Slimène, whom she had charged with buying her an outfit, she could not afford women's attire:

> You know nothing of what it *costs* to dress *not well,* but at least pass-ably as a Frenchwoman: a wig (this costs, for a shaved head like mine, some 15 to 20 francs, because a simple plait won't do), a hat, underwear, corset, petticoats, skirts, stockings, shoes, gloves and so on. All I will concede is to stop *dressing as an Arab,* which is anyway the only thing which would prejudice the authorities against me.[32]

After the trial in June, for which she finally decided to wear native women's clothing, Eberhardt was kicked out of Algeria again. During her exile in Marseille, she met Lydie Paschkoff, who had been sending her flamboyantly overwrought letters. She was back in Algeria in January 1902 and made the acquaintance of Colonel Lyautey, one of the architects of colonial Africa, who appreciated her deep knowledge of Algeria. While working for him, ostensibly to report on an area known as the Sud-Oranais, she arrived in Aïn Sefra, where she fell ill enough to be hospitalized for a few days. On 21 October 1904, shortly after she checked out of the hospital, Eberhardt was swept up in a flash flood and drowned at the age of twenty-eight.[33]

WEST AFRICA

West Africa was brought to Europe's attention by the Portuguese, who, in the fifteenth century, were mapping its coastline as part of their efforts to find a way around it. When they, along with English, French and Spanish, settled there, systematic survey and exploration commenced. One of the consequences of this knowledge was brutal and unforeseen: the slave trade, which had until then been limited to Africa, spread to Europe and the colonies of the New World.

Slaves had been carried to the Americas from the beginning of the sixteenth century. By the end of the eighteenth century, many who had escaped during the American War of Independence chose to go back to their ancestral homeland: Sierra Leone, or "The Province of Freedom" as it had been called, was created for this purpose by British abolitionists. The settlement, scattered about on parcels of poor land, suffered from a high rate of mortality. Supplies were scarce and self-sufficiency almost unachievable.

Early in 1791, twenty-five-year-old Bristol native Anna Maria Falconbridge found herself on a ship bound for Sierra Leone. She was with her husband, Alexander, a surgeon who had served on slavers and who was now heading a relief team. Her *Narrative of Two Voyages to the River Sierra Leone, During the Years 1791–2–3* (1794) may have been the first published account of Sierra Leone by an Englishwoman. She wrote frankly for the time, spilling the then-shocking details of Englishwomen living with the freed blacks and of her first sight of a dreadful slave compound. She didn't gloss over her husband's hot temper and tendency to intemperance; both qualities cost him his job. The Falconbridges were recalled at the end of 1792, but before they could return to England, Alexander, already ill with fever, drank himself into a stupor and died on 28 December 1792.

Anna almost immediately married Isaac DuBois, a white Loyalist from North Carolina, on 7 January 1793. The couple returned to England in June via Jamaica, their first leg on a slaver. She was agreeably surprised to see how well the slaves were treated; they ate decently, their spacious quarters were clean and the only death occurred to a young man who had been sick before departure. The captain may have been on his best behaviour, knowing that Anna was penning a memoir. If so, his efforts paid

Freetown, from a distance.
A. de Bar, *Tour du monde* 26, 1873: 356.

off; she was pleased to say a few words on the benefits of slavery.[34] She spent the next few years trying to
get compensation for monies owed to her and her
late husband. Her book was part of that campaign, but of its author
nothing more is known.

The waters off Senegal were the site of the wreck of the
Medusa in 1816, immortalized by Théodore Géricault. The region
had been fought over by France and Britain and was, theoretically,
a French possession, though the English were unwilling to give it
up. The Picard family★ was on the *Medusa,* and the account of the
family's sufferings was published by Mlle Picard, who later became
Mme Dard. Another account was published by two soldiers,
Savigny and Corréard.

The family, consisting of about ten members, sailed from
Rochefort to West Africa in a convoy of four ships, one of which
was the *Medusa,* transporting some 150 soldiers; another carried
the French governor and his family. Somewhere below the Tropic
of Cancer, the captain admitted he had no idea where he was. An
"imposter" took over, claiming familiarity with the waters, and
grounded the *Medusa*. The soldiers on board, including Savigny
and Corréard, as well as the wife of one of them, were put onto a
flimsy raft with only one sack of water-soaked biscuits. Another
ship was designated to tow the raft, and after much pleading, the

---

★ I have found nothing to indicate that they were related to Aurélie Picard.

Picards, whom the governor had declined to help, managed to get onto that. They were horror-struck when their ship abandoned the raft. That Savigny and Corréard managed to survive was nothing short of miraculous.

The Picards and their ship made it to land, a section of barren coast somewhere off St. Louis (also known as Senegal). They formed a ragged caravan and began marching. The Picard women and children moved slowly (they had lost their shoes on landing), so some of the party suggested leaving them behind; fortunately, they were under the protection of a sympathetic officer. Eventually, the survivors fell in with a small group of Arabs, who escorted them to safety.

The Picards settled at St. Louis, but their fortunes went from bad to worse; in November Mme Picard died; M Picard lost his post as attorney and made an ill-fated stab at commerce. He then tried farming on the insalubrious island of Safal. Of their bad luck, Mlle Picard wrote, "We were the most miserable creatures that ever existed on the face of the earth . . . [We regretted] a hundred times we had not perished in the shipwreck."[35]

Fever carried away the youngest child, then M Picard died in August 1819. At last salvation came, in the form of M Dard, an old family friend and director of the French school. He adopted the ragged family, married Mlle Picard and took them back to France.

Seventy-four years later, Mary Kingsley—spinster, self-taught scholar, dutiful daughter of recently deceased parents and obliging sister to a lazy, ungrateful brother—packed her bags and caught a steamer for Sierra Leone. She had spent her first thirty years caring for her invalid mother and lacked even a basic formal education, and there she was, heading off to one of the most notoriously dangerous regions of the world ostensibly to explore and study "fish and fetish."[36] Spurning hammocks, tents and porters, she made two major excursions in as many years, using the cover of trader to justify her presence. On the surface, nothing could be more absurd.

In fact, Mary's background prepared her amply for these undertakings. Her father, George Kingsley, brother of the novelists Charles and Henry, was himself an inveterate traveller; he had left home only weeks after marrying his pregnant cook four days before Mary was born. He came back long enough to sire another child, Charley, then was off again.[37]

Deprived of orthodox schooling, Kingsley turned to her father's huge library and devoured it all: classics, philosophy, ethnography, natural history and travellers' tales. Her knowledge of and interest in West Africa was fostered by readings of the great explorers Richard Burton, Paul Du Chaillu and Pierre de Brazza.[38]

By the time Kingsley's parents died, Charley was off wandering, coming home intermittently. Mary resolved to take care of him whenever he returned and planned her trips around his timetable. Her first real escape came in 1892, when she went to the Canary Islands. From there she got a glimpse of Africa and decided it would be her next destination. A year later she was on board the *Lagos,* a cockroach-infested trading ship, where she was regaled with reports of those lost to fever. The ship's first stop was Freetown. It then proceeded to Accra; Bonny, in present-day Nigeria; and São Paulo de Loanda (Luanda), in Angola. From this southernmost point Kingsley worked her way back north, passing through Congo Free State, Congo Français and Cameroon, to Calabar, where she caught the *Rochelle* back to Liverpool.[39]

When she arrived home in January 1894, laden with fish specimens, mounted insects, fetish objects and photographic plates, Kingsley began assembling writings her father had started for a book that was destined to become *Notes on Sport and Travel.* She also made the acquaintance of one of her heroes, ichthyologist Albert Charles Günther, and she began preparing for another trip to West Africa.[40]

Mary Kingsley. Photo by A. G. Dew-Smith, in *Memories* by Edward Clodd, London: Chapman and Hall, 1916, frontispiece.

➳"The climate is unhealthy, so that the usual make of Englishman does not like to take his wife out to the coast with him."—Mary Kingsley[41]

Ogooué River, Gabon.
A. de Bar, *Tour du monde* 31, 1876: 273.

Kingsley left in December 1894 on her second expedition. Her eventual destination was Gabon, where she paddled up the Ogooué River to study the Fang populations deep in the forest. Again in her guise of trader, laden with toothbrushes, handkerchiefs and tobacco, she defied common sense, became even more independent by learning how to handle a canoe and was probably the first white woman to climb Mount Cameroon, which had thwarted many other travellers.[43]

Returning to England in November 1895, Kingsley set to work on her *Travels in West Africa,* which was published in January 1897. It was wildly successful, considering that it was a treatise of 630 pages, plus appendices, filled with incomprehensible place names and customs. But it was enlivened by a self-deprecating, hilarious style. Kingsley herself called the book a "word swamp." Some reviews were condescendingly enthusiastic; the *Daily Chronicle* wrote, "There is something so quaint about Miss Kingsley's diction, so irresistibly comical is her way of looking at things, so kind and gentle and womanly is she through it all, that the big volume before us can scarcely fail to please anybody." However, *Nature,* in solemn tones, declared that "[it] stands alone as a vivid picture of West African life by a writer whose point of view is as nearly impartial as

"Africa is an alarming place to walk about in at night, both for a witch doctor who believes in all his local forest devils, and a lady who believes in all the local material ones."
—Mary Kingsley[42]

we can ever hope to see."[44] The equally ambitious *West African Studies* followed in 1899.

Mary Kingsley's contradictions could fill a book. Her health in England was poor—she suffered from rheumatism and migraines, among other ailments— but once on African soil, surrounded by tropical diseases, she thrived. She collected valuable ethnographic and zoological material—several species of fish were named after her—but claimed that her own work was fraught with error and was scarcely authoritative. She wore Victorian stays and awkward long, thick skirts in the hot, humid climate while fording rivers, tipping canoes and falling into trappers' pits. She was a product of a conservative age, yet she defended the liquor trade to Africans, supported polygamy and condemned the activities of missionaries. She was more independent than many Western women of today but decried feminism, flatly denouncing attempts by women to attain equality with men. Although resolutely feminine she often referred to herself as a man, writing in *West African Studies,* "I am not a literary man, only a student of West Africa," and "I am not by nature a commercial man myself."[45]

> "West Africa probably will never be a pleasant place wherein to spend the winter months, a holiday ground that will serve to recuperate the jaded energies of our poets and painters, like the Alps or Italy."
> —Mary Kingsley[47]

Kingsley was also shy and awkward, yet she entertained crowds of up to two thousand people who came to hear her terrifyingly exciting experiences delivered with dropped "Hs" in her mordantly witty voice. She spoke to the Royal Scottish Geographical Society; was present while a male stand-in gave her lecture to the Liverpool Geographical Society; and was ignored by London's Royal Geographical Society, as women at that time were then excluded from that learned group.[46]

Kingsley was not able to return to West Africa as she wished. Instead, on 10 March 1900, she boarded the *Moor* for Cape Town to help nurse injured Boer War soldiers. But the demands were too much even for Mary Kingsley. She died of heart failure on 3 June 1900, the result of typhoid fever, and was buried at sea.

Arabia to Persia
A Desire for Danger

THE TWO RIDERS DISMOUNTED, tied their horses to the low bush in front of them, then looked out across the barren desert. Low, rocky mounds and twisted, wind-blown shrubs extended unbroken as far as the eye could see. They had just sat down to rest when a low, thudding sound broke the silence. Suddenly, one of them yelled, "Get on your mare. This is a *ghazú!*" In an instant, Anne and Wilfrid Blunt were in the midst of a Bedouin raid that had seemingly materialized out of nowhere. But Anne, who had sprained her knee a few days earlier, couldn't move quickly enough and was knocked down by the blow of a spear. One of the raiders grabbed Wilfrid's rifle and smacked him on the head with it. Anne cried out in Arabic, "I am under your protection." Only then did the bandits, members of the Roala tribe, realize that they had just attacked a woman. They stopped, dumbfounded. A short while later, they were all sitting together sharing dates, the Roala as guests of their intended victims.[1]

This was January 1879, and the Blunts were on their expedition through the Arabian desert, the Nejd. A year earlier, they had been in Syria, and after a brief return to England, they were back in Damascus, preparing to head south into Arabia. Accompanied by Mohammed and Hanna, who had been with them on their trek through Syria, they left on 13 December, only a week after they arrived. Their route alternated between grassy plain and inhospitable, rocky desert. Raging sandstorms slowed their progress. Then, near Kaf, just inside present-day Saudi Arabia, Anne fell off her horse and sprained her knee. After their tumultuous introduction to the Roala, they made their way to Al Jawf, then Hail, where they were hospitably received by Emir Mohammed ibn Rashid. After a week there, they joined a Persian pilgrim caravan that was passing through on its way north to Meshhed Ali (An Najaf), south of Baghdad. Their progress was slow and

Anne and Wilfrid Blunt. When asked if she was afraid of being attacked, Anne Blunt replied, "Whatever my feelings I should certainly not be such a fool as to show or confess to any sort of fear."[2]

G. Vuillier, *Tour du monde* 43, 1882: 1.

Targets of a ghazú, or raid, Anne Blunt is on the ground, uncomfortably close to the tip of a spear, while Wilfrid has just been smacked in the head with his rifle.

G. Vuillier, *Tour du monde* 43, 1882: 13.

monotonous—they ran short of food and resented the caravan leader's efforts to extort more money out of everyone—but they eventually made it. Keen to continue, they pressed on through Persia to India. From these adventures, Anne wrote *A Pilgrimage to Nejd,* which, like her earlier book, was edited by Wilfrid.

Arabia, Persia and Mesopotamia, isolated from European influence longer than the Levant, maintained rigorous control over women's ability to travel openly. Most women didn't even try to travel through this area; the thinly inhabited, harsh terrain and the searing heat that alternated with the freezing cold were discouraging. Nonetheless, these regions were desired by British, French, Russian and Turkish governments at various periods, and the attention inevitably brought travellers.

Mesopotamia, present-day Iraq, was usually reached from Syria or the Persian Gulf. When the Blunts made it to Baghdad in 1878, they found an ugly town, shrunken "like a withered nut inside its shell" with little to hint at its days of splendour.[3] Ida Pfeiffer, one

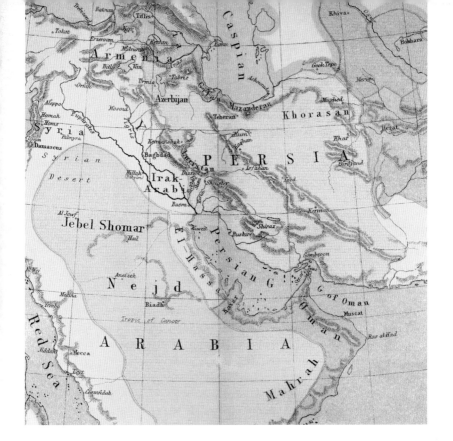

Western Asia.
Philips' Handy Atlas, c. 1897.

of the first women travellers to write about Baghdad, had much the same impression.

Pfeiffer arrived there in 1848, as part of her monumental first journey round the world. She had sailed from Bombay to Basra via Muscat, spending eighteen days on deck suffering from bilious fever, as the smallpox seething below carried off three passengers. From Basra, she sailed up the Tigris. Although she was warned against appearing without a veil, she couldn't stand the suffocating garment and chose to wear only an *isar,* a voluminous linen wrapper, topped with a fez wrapped with cloth.[4]

Indecent conversations and behaviour at the Baghdad harems and baths shocked Pfeiffer, though she didn't specify what happened to provoke such a response. Otherwise, she was overwhelmed by the hospitality shown to her; travelling permits were granted without hesitation; food and places to sleep were willingly offered. In the blazing June heat, she joined a caravan and journeyed fourteen days to Mosul, travelling "like the poorest Arab." While there, she detoured to Layard's excavations at Nimrud, then arranged to go to Tabriz. Of this trek she wrote, "I

"A Migrating Horde of Tartars." An artist's impression of Ida Pfeiffer hurtling through the Mesopotamian countryside.
Pfeiffer c. 1851, facing p. 208.

started on this journey with some feelings of anxiety, and scarcely dared to hope for a fortunate termination. On that account I sent my papers and manuscripts from here to Europe, so that in case I was robbed or murdered my diary would at least come into the hands of my sons." This parcel took over a year and a half to make its way to Austria.[5]

She was temporarily delayed at Ruwandiz, where the local head merchant refused to help her go farther, explaining that no caravans were departing and that to travel alone would mean that she'd be "shot or beheaded." Nonplussed, she wangled a guide and a horse and safely made it to the town of Oromia (Urmia), about eighty kilometres on, where she stayed with missionaries until she was able to arrange the next stage. Upon her arrival at Tabriz, a startled European asked her:

> "How did you come here, alone? Have you been robbed? Have you parted from your company and only left them in the town?" . . .
> He thought it bordered on the fabulous that a woman should have

succeeded, without any knowledge of the language, in penetrating through such countries and such people. I also could not be too thankful for the evident protection which Providence had afforded me. I felt myself as happy and lively as if I had taken a new lease of my life.[6]

Pfeiffer's onward journey into Asiatic Russia was soured by surly, hard-drinking Russians and by a misunderstanding that led to her being kidnapped by two zealous and suspicious guards. She was released after an uncomfortable overnight stay in a post house, then continued west to the Crimea. Her further travels were cut short by the news that revolution had broken out in Austria; in October 1848, Pfeiffer finally went home.

Rather than travel through Persia imprisoned in a suffocating chador, Jane Dieulafoy chose to go *en cavalier,* dressed as a horseman. "Horseboy" would be more descriptive, as the thirty-year-old Frenchwoman was slim and, naturally, smooth-faced. She and her husband, engineer Marcel Dieulafoy, made two expeditions to Persia, the first, in 1881–82, an archaeological reconnaissance from the Black Sea to the Persian Gulf and the second, in 1884–86, to conduct excavations at Susa. Jane wrote about both expeditions in the *Tour du monde* (1883 and 1887). They were succinct accounts enlivened by vigorous observations of the day-to-day pleasures and pains of travelling in Persia.

Before the couple headed east, Jane had already tested her stamina when, as a newly married twenty-year-old, she had accompanied her husband, then an officer, to the front of the Franco-Prussian War. They had also toured Spain, Morocco, Algeria and Upper Egypt.[7]

Their first Persian trip took them to Tabriz, Isfahan and Shiraz and through Mesopotamia to Baghdad. Staying in dank, windowless chambers in lowly caravanserais and travelling with a minimum of equipment, they were constantly on the move as they made notes, took pictures, surveyed for possible

Jane Dieulafoy. Dronsart, 54.

sites to excavate and dealt diplomatically with functionaries. Their survey included the city of Susa, which had been partially excavated in 1851 by William Loftus. Numerous enticing mounds still awaited exploration.

While in Kashan, Jane took her camera to the bazaar, but the townsfolk objected to having their photos taken and a fracas broke out around her. Marcel thought it best—as a face-saving measure—to immediately complain of ill treatment to the governor. The consequences were unexpected but delightful. The governor's wife, hearing that the photographer in question was a woman, sneaked over dressed in a servant's veil to have her picture taken.

The Dieulafoys left Persia in 1882, feeling sick and tired and

Jane Dieulafoy, confronting bandits as she protects the expedition's supplies and equipment. The original caption read, "I have fourteen balls at your disposal; go find six more friends!"[8] Tofani, from a sketch by Marcel Dieulafoy, *Tour du monde* 55, 1887: 35.

wanting nothing but to stay home. After six months of cooling their heels, however, both were ready to take off again, eager to know what the mounds at Susa might hold. After complex negotiations, they were on their way at the end of 1884. They sailed from Marseille through the Suez to Aden. From there they went up the Persian Gulf to the mouth of the Karun River. They arrived at Susa seventy-one days after leaving France.

It took only a few days to organize diggers, and soon they made their first big find, a faience pavement of a lion. The following spring they briefly returned

Jane Dieulafoy, left. She, her husband, and two fellow scholars were confined to their tent for two days because of bad weather.
Myrbach, Tour du monde 55, 1887: 25.

to France, where they found that Persian opposition to their work had been communicated to the French government, but they were again given the green light to continue. Back in Persia, they divided their time between excavating and exploring the countryside. The diggers unearthed a spectacular faience wall, which turned out to be the Frieze of the Archers, a significant piece of Achaemenid art. After they returned again to France in 1886, Jane continued to write; her articles on Spain were published in the *Tour du monde* from 1900 to 1907.

Isabella Bird's account of her year-long journey through Persia and the vaguely defined region of Kurdistan (adjoining areas of Turkey, Syria, Iran and Iraq) in 1890 was published as *Journeys in Persia and Kurdistan* (1891). She travelled, at times alone, but sometimes in the company of Major Herbert Sawyer (referred to, diplomatically, as M——), who was surveying the region for political reasons. The fiercely independent Bird was unhappy to have to curtail her liberty, but rumoured difficulties forced her to accept that she would have to go with an escort or not at all. She visited cities such as Tehran and Qom and spent three and a half months in Bakhtiari country in central Persia.

Aiming first for Tehran, she, Sawyer and her opium-addicted Gulf Arab servant, Hadji Hussein, set out from Baghdad (which she found agreeable) in January with a caravan. She wore two holsters, one of which housed a revolver and a tea-making set, the other milk and dates. She also sported a cork helmet, a mask and an "American mountain dress," covered by a jacket, and tan boots. Bird and her companions stayed in freezing, damp and filthy caravanserais, somehow succeeded in floundering through deep snow across windswept wastelands and survived a potentially disastrous accident with their mules and baggage.⁹

> "I see endless difficulties ahead, and a prospect of illustrating in my own experience the *dictum* often dinned into my ears, that 'No lady ought to travel alone in Persia.'"—Isabella Bird¹¹

The fifty-nine-year-old Bird was encumbered by an agonizing spinal affliction. She initially rode a mule until pain forced her to try a horse; it's doubtful she would have been able to continue otherwise. The trip was harder than anything she had ever undertaken; her tenacity and fortitude were simply unparalleled.

Although Bird veiled herself in public, she was nonetheless the target of insults and jeering, even in large towns such as Kermanshah and Isfahan. The pandemonium that seemed always to surround her increased during rest stops, when crowds of ailing people came to benefit from her medical kit. Her expertise was sought for eye ailments, rheumatism, deafness and even moribund love lives. In spite of her generosity of time and medicines, she was robbed several times of money, animals and essential gear. At one village, the people were pressed by their chief to pay back, from their own pockets, stolen money.

The hardships were many, but so were the pleasures. Her Persian interpreter, Mirza Yusuf, became an invaluable companion; she exulted in her sense of freedom; and she became so thoroughly attached to her Persian horse, Boy, that she was loath to part with him at her journey's end, the Turkish city of Trebizond. When she reached that city in December 1890, she stood looking at the Black Sea and thought, "Such is the magic charm of Asia that I would willingly have turned back at that moment to the snowy plateaux of Armenia and the savage mountains of Kurdistan."¹⁰

Madame Dieulafoy. — Dessin de É. Bayard, d'après une photographie.

Lambs in Wolves' Clothing

MANY WOMEN TRAVELLERS FOUND IT PRACTICAL to disguise themselves as men, especially in countries where women were forbidden to travel. Men's clothing was also useful for climbing mountains, riding horseback and other physical pursuits. But no matter how appropriate such dress might have been, it was considered perverse to flaunt the disapproved apparel, among certain women at least. Frenchwomen were far more nonchalant about "cross-dressing" than their British counterparts—not surprising, considering their role model, George Sand (also a traveller), who pioneered such attire. Mary Seacole, from her vantage point on the Isthmus of Panama, was probably thinking of Sand when she wrote, "Those French lady writers who desire to enjoy the privileges of man, with the irresponsibility of the other sex, would have been delighted with the disciples who were carrying their principles into practice in the streets of Cruces."[1]

Women such as Catalina de Erauso, Jeanne Baret and Rose de Freycinet wore men's clothing long before Sand donned her pants. The Spanish-born Erauso, also known as "La Monja Alferez" (the Lieutenant Nun), lived in the seventeenth century and fully adopted a male persona, changing her name to Antonio, taking women lovers and voyaging as an officer to Peru, Chile and Argentina. Her sex was eventually revealed, and though she had been respected as a man, she became an outcast in her ambiguous new identity.[2]

Baret worked as a "male" domestic for the naturalist Philibert Commerson and in 1766 accompanied him as his valet on Bougainville's round-the-world expedition. If Commerson was aware that this twenty-six-year-old he was a she, he didn't let on. Although rumours circulated among the sailors—after all, she was beardless and slightly built—her sex was only finally revealed in Tahiti by Tahitians, who recognized her as a woman the moment she disembarked. From then

ABOVE, BACKGROUND: *Catalina de Erauso.* Cortambert, 15.

FACING PAGE: *Jane Dieulafoy, dressed as a horseman.* Émile Bayard, *Tour du monde* 4, 1883: 137.

on the sailors no longer treated her as one of the guys, but she continued to assist Commerson and became a skilled botanist.[3]

Rose de Freycinet, wife of Louis Claude Desaules de Freycinet, briefly wore masculine attire to sneak onto her husband's frigate *L'Uranie* in 1817, defying regulations that forbade women on French government ships.[4]

There were many more: Olympe d'Audouard, Adèle Hommaire de Hell and Maria de Ujfalvy-Bourbon were all proud of their trousers. However, nineteenth-century French law made it illegal for women to wear men's clothing in public unless they needed to do so for their health—a stipulation that seemed flexible—so Jane Dieulafoy, among others, applied for and received *permission de travestissement*.[5]

Isabel Burton relished the freedom that men's clothing gave her during her sojourn in Syria: "So attired I could . . . enter all the places which women are not deemed worthy to see. My chief difficulty was that my toilet always had to be performed in the dead of night." She forgot herself on occasion, however, and sent women in harems running in panic when she inadvertently swaggered in, disguised in male attire.[6]

For Laurence Hope, dressing as a Pathan boy was a means of staying with her husband. For Isabel Gunn, cross-dressing meant she could go to Canada and work at a Hudson's Bay Company fort. Dr. James Miranda Stuart Barry, an Edinburgh physician, adopted a male persona, served in the Crimean War and later became inspector general of hospitals in Upper Canada. Isabelle Eberhardt sported masculine clothing as a girl, and she never fully gave in to dressing as a woman. She went a step further when she transformed herself into an Algerian man, taking a man's name, wearing male garb and participating in religious rituals only open to Muslim men.

Ida Pfeiffer had been advised to dress as a man for her journey through the Holy Land, but all she had to do was look at herself to see how ridiculous the result would be. She wrote that "my short, spare figure would have seemed to belong to a youth, and my face to an old man." So she outfitted herself in a blouse and Turkish trousers, and was treated with respect throughout her voyage, though women thought her hair, which she cut short for convenience' sake, odd.[7]

Women who wore men's clothes were scorned by those who thought such actions beneath them. Emily Beaufort was critical of an American woman who had deceived the monks of Mar Saba, a monastery in Palestine open only to men. "[She] entered the monastery in men's clothes, concealing her hands in her pockets while going over the whole building, but whilst taking coffee, her sex was discovered, and she was immediately expelled by the justly offended monks. To say nothing of the breach of good faith in such an act, one consoles oneself by reflecting, that, though taken for a man, she could not have been mistaken for a gentleman."[8]

Numerous women went "native," especially in the Middle East, though few thought they were fooling anyone. Hester Stanhope, dressed as an Arab man, had entered the Mar Antonius, a monastery, like Mar Saba, forbidden to females. She rode her she-ass into the hall and visited the whole place; the monks were hysterical—they spouted the legend that any woman who crossed the threshold would have a "ghastly accident," but nothing happened to her. It helped, probably, that male members of her party followed her to make sure the monks did not attack her. Anne Blunt wore Bedouin clothing, as did Jane Digby el-Mezrab, though Digby, through her immersion in Syrian life, had very much earned the right to do so.

Harriet Martineau was doubtful that oriental dress would achieve anything but ridicule. "An Englishwoman," she claimed, "can never, in a mere passage through an Eastern country, make herself look like an Eastern woman; and an unsupported assumption of any native custom will obtain for her no respect, but only make her appear ashamed of her own origin and ways."[9]

India
Forgetting to Be Shocked

WHEN WE LEFT ELIZA FAY SETTING OUT FOR SUEZ, where she and her husband, Anthony, were to board a ship bound for India, she was terrified to think what fate might have in store for her. Marauding bandits had been stripping European travellers bare. Luckily, the couple reached Suez unharmed, though she declared they'd been robbed of everything. When they arrived in Calicut in November 1779, however, their ship was immediately surrounded by hostile boats belonging to ruler Hyder Ali, who was in conflict with the British. One of the ladies on board, a Mrs. Tulloh, who had frequently "expressed a violent desire for some species of adventure," brought her chair up on deck to watch, saying it was "the next best thing to escaping from shipwreck."[1]

A misunderstanding had forced the hasty departure of the British consul, leaving only the Danes representing Europe. Without their country's protection, the Fays, who had intended to carry on to Calcutta anyway, decided to remain on board. Most of the other passengers disembarked. On the heels of a rumour that the English were going to attack Calicut, the ship was boarded by a large party of sepoys, led by a Captain Ayres, a former highwayman, now a mercenary in Hyder Ali's employ. Claiming that they were there to protect the passengers, the soldiers plundered them instead. The Fays pled poverty, hiding three valuable gold watches in Eliza's hair, first stopping their works with pins so that the ticking wouldn't give them away.

Allowed only a few essentials, they were taken ashore and imprisoned in the English factory, which had been sacked. The other passengers, who had left the boat earlier, were suddenly rounded up and thrown in with them. All were held for ransom. The Fays scraped together enough money to buy their release and two passports, identifying them as Frenchmen. To effect this masquerade, Eliza wore a nankeen jacket, a pair of striped trousers, a night cap, a "*mighty*

"An Afternoon in the Himalayas." The two women on the right are being carried in a hammock-like contraption known as a dandy.
Graphic, 25 September 1880: cover.

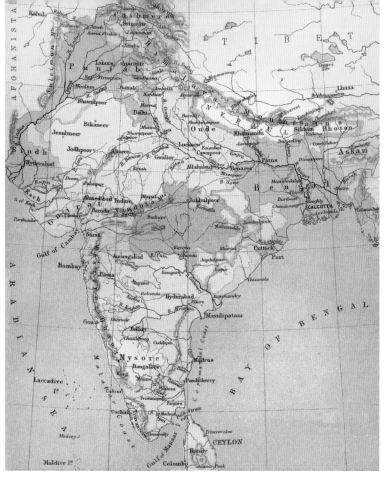

India. Philips' Handy Atlas, c. 1897.

smart hat" and a pair of Anthony's shoes. Her husband declared that she looked just like her father.[2] In spite of the clever disguise, their escape effort failed, and they had to cough up more money. On 21 January 1780, they were finally on their way to Calcutta.

Anthony Fay had proven to be an imbecile, misjudging situations and generally mucking up their journey. Eliza stuck it out with him for ten more years, then left him when he disgraced himself by running into debt, alienating their friends and fathering an illegitimate child. She wrote *Original Letters from India: Containing a Narrative of a Journey Through Egypt, and the Author's Imprisonment at Calicut by Hyder Ally: 1779–1815* (1817), lost money at various ill-conceived ventures and travelled between England and India two more times, as well as to New York. She died in Calcutta in 1816, at the age of sixty.

India, with its cotton, silk, jewels, drugs and spices, had been a trading partner, via the Levant, with Europe for centuries. Direct trade was established with the opening of the sea route around the Cape of Good Hope by Vasco da Gama in 1498, though Portugal managed to maintain a monopoly until 1600, when it was broken by the Dutch. The British, French and Danish were also anxious to get a piece of the trade pie and each formed trading companies; the British had the East India Company, the French the Compagnie des Indes Orientales, and so on. The convergence of trade rivals led to fighting, both on land and at sea, as each tried to gain control. There were also various Indian rulers to negotiate with, as India was not a cohesively governed country. The delicate transactions were often unsuccessful and led to violence between Europeans and Indians.

By the 1680s, the British had settled at Bombay (Mumbai), Madras and Calcutta and the French at Pondicherry and Chandernagore. But by 1765, Britain had become the dominant power in India, flooding the country with soldiers and administrators. Initially, the salaries given to these expatriates were inadequate to support wives, but this situation changed rapidly. British wives became highly sought after, especially in Calcutta, where the marriage market was firmly established and "regularly replenished with hopeful single females."[3] High wages and low living costs allowed luxurious lifestyles not attainable in Britain.

Maria Graham, who would go on to write about South America, described her stay in India from 1809 to 1811 in *Journal of a Residence in India* (1812). Her disapproval of the other Englishwomen there is clear from her statement that they were "under-bred and over-dressed and, with the exception of one or two, very ignorant and very grossière."[4] This pronouncement may not have been entirely fair, but most Englishwomen in India did not make much effort to learn about, or adapt to, their new home. Their tightly knit communities shielded them from almost every aspect of Indian life except heat, disease and bugs. Few Englishwomen tolerated close contact with Indians, a repugnance that was reciprocated, especially by the caste-conscious Hindus. The Sikhs, too, were inclined to disdain the company of European females.

Fanny Parks was exceptional in her ability and willingness to circulate between cultures. In 1822, she and her husband, Charles Parks, a writer, or clerk, for the East India Company, went to

CURRY & RICE

(ON FORTY PLATES)

OR

THE INGREDIENTS OF SOCIAL LIFE

AT

"OUR STATION" IN INDIA

BY CAPT? GEO. F. ATKINSON.

LONDON.

JOHN B. DAY, LITHOGRAPHER, PRINTER & PUBLISHER,

2, SAVOY STREET, STRAND

Calcutta. Four years later he was posted to Allahabad and, except for a brief transfer to Cawnpore (Kanpur) and a leave of absence at the Cape, stayed there until he retired in 1846. Fanny, in principle, accompanied him, but she mainly travelled, sometimes alone, sometimes with companions. She littered her two-volume account, *Wanderings of a Pilgrim in Search of the Picturesque* (1850), with Hindustani words and became adept enough in the language to act as an interpreter. Her name on the title page appears in Persian only, leading some to describe the book as having been published anonymously.

فاني پاركس

Isabella Fane and Emily Eden were in India at the same time as Parks. Whereas Parks was far more interested in what was going on in the zenana, or harem, than in Anglo homes, Fane and Eden revealed how the bulk of British women lived. During the cooler season they went visiting, studied the latest fashion news from Europe, planned alarmingly large dinners and almost expired from heat, mosquitoes or dysentery. Households were huge, swollen to immense proportions by servants; Fane's had sixty-seven. Every woman had a maid; even the maids had maids. Come October's high temperatures, households would pack up and head to the hill station of Simla in Kashmir, where the cool mountain air made life bearable.

Fane, the illegitimate daughter of commander in chief of India Henry Fane,★ dished the dirt on Anglo society, thanks in part to her exalted position as her father's hostess in Calcutta. Caustic observations drip off the pages of her letters; insults fly; disrespectful pronouncements accompany every description of persons and sights. She would probably be delighted to know that we have read that Emily Eden and her sister Fanny "are both great talkers, both old, both ugly and both s—k like polecats!" Or that the rajah of Bharatpur's exposed breast was an object never to be forgotten: "this machine of his hung down more than the biggest of ladies'. *I* should have been proud to have *half* as much, but very sorry to have possessed the whole!" Fane could have become a new Montagu, as she seemed unable to refrain from

Curry & Rice, n.d., by Captain George F. Atkinson, took a light-hearted view of Anglo life in India. This title page shows a young woman perched sidesaddle, with her attendants and an officer companion.

★ Fane's parents had never married as a result of her father's previous marriage (her mother had returned to England), but this did not seem to affect her position in society.[5]

commenting on even the most personal or gruesome events. About a river trip in February 1836, she wrote of her amusement at the spectacle of the dead floating down the Ganges: "My curiosity (laudable!!) was satisfied, for I saw many good specimens—particularly on our return, for one fine whole man floated past the window of the cabin at which I was standing."[6]

Fane, who wouldn't have turned down a chance to get married, was broken-hearted when a sympathetic companion, the widower Mr. Beresford, married her cousin. At the age of thirty-four, with her father now retired and estranged from her mother, Fane was relegated to the periphery of the society she had so mocked. Rootless, she returned to Europe and lived mostly in France, where she died in 1886.[7]

Although Fane had ridiculed the Edens, she liked them a lot. They both left accounts, but only Emily's was published in her lifetime. This was called *Up the Country* (1866), a record of her travels with Fanny and her brother, Governor-General Lord Auckland, from Calcutta to Kashmir from 1837 to 1840. Their huge party left Calcutta by steamer in October 1837 and sailed along the Ganges as far as Benares, then travelled the rest of the way by land, riding horses, elephants and mules, walking or being carried in various contraptions. For the most part they camped, though occasionally they stayed in government houses. Their route took them through Patna, where they toured the opium factories; Dinapore, Benares (Varanasi), Allahabad, Fatehpur and Cawnpore, near where they viewed the miserable evidence of famine; Lucknow, Delhi and Simla. Eden's spelling is at times unique, especially of place names, and she rarely bothered to correct her mistakes. Like Fane, she had an unrestrained zest to her writing, leading one reader, Lucie Duff Gordon, to dismiss it as a kind of "theatre burlesque view of the customs of a strange country."[8]

No matter how superficial her idea of India was, Eden's streak of realism allowed her to consider how galled locals must have been by the excess and frivolity of Europeans at Simla. "I sometimes wonder," she wrote, "they do not cut all our heads off, and say nothing more about it." Still, she was miffed at being slighted by Sikh men: "The poor ignorant creatures are perfectly unconscious what a very superior article an Englishwoman is. They think us contemptible, if anything, which is a mistake."[9]

Both Fane and Eden were ungrateful guests of Maharaja Ranjit Singh, the ruler of Amritsar, in Kashmir. Fane wrote of a dinner in 1837 that "because I was the great man's daughter [Ranjit] fed me with his own fingers, through the *hands* of another, with quail curry, which after pretending to taste I deposited into Captain Hay's glove, prepared for the purpose." Eden had a similar tale. She managed to dispose of "two broiled quails, an apple, a pear, a great lump of sweetmeat, and some pomegranate-seeds."[10] Eden, perhaps, could be forgiven; she was often ill.

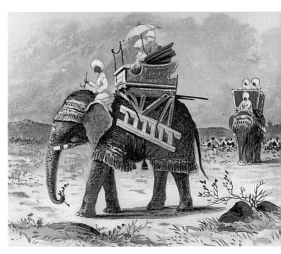

Lady Annie Brassey and her family "en route to hunt black buck with cheetahs, Hyderabad." Brassey 1889.

At Simla, Eden met the exotic Spanish dancer Lola Montez, before Montez learned how to dance and before she became Spanish. At this point her name was Eliza James, née Gilbert, she was seventeen and she was with her handsome new thirty-year-old husband, Lieutenant Thomas James. Earlier, in England, her mother had mistakenly introduced him to Eliza. In no time, Thomas seduced the girl, ran away with her to Ireland, then married her. In September 1839, when his leave was up, the couple sailed for Calcutta. Eden was quite enamoured of Eliza's beauty but forecast trouble for the newlyweds.[11] But James/Montez must wait.

Simla was a hotbed for affairs, since many women were there without their husbands and officers were there without their wives, if they had any. The plethora of unattached young women meant that chaperoning was a thriving business. Eden wrote that just looking at a man for a second too long meant that one was interested, and dancing with him more than once was tantamount to a declaration of engagement. Anne Blunt made a tactical error by letting Wilfrid loose in Simla in 1879; he immediately got in hot water by courting a Mrs. Batten, who later became one of his lovers.[12]

The Taj Mahal, as illustrated in Ida Pfeiffer's A Woman's Journey Round the World, *c. 1851, facing p. 179.*

Women who lived in India have done a good job crowding out those who simply travelled. One of the latter was Ida Pfeiffer, who landed at Ceylon in 1847 as part of her first round-the-world tour. She had come from Hong Kong via Singapore to Ceylon, then went on to Madras, Calcutta and Benares. Her seven-week trip from Delhi to Bombay, with a succession of Indian drivers and guides as her only company, was highly unusual. Her transport was by oxen and wagon or by camel; she slept either in caravansarais with other Indian travellers or at the homes of resident agents. In February 1848, she landed in the town of Rumtscha (south of Kotah), which had no accommodation, and she had to make her bed on an open veranda. She finally vented some of the frustrations of travel: "Half of the inhabitants of the town gathered round me, and watched all my motions and doings with the greatest attention. I afforded them an opportunity of studying the appearance of an angry European female."[13]

Marianne North and Constance Gordon Cumming also devoted a great deal of time to India. North was there from 1877 to 1879 and left no corner of the country unexplored. Gordon Cumming's *In the Himalayas and on the Indian Plains* (1884) answered the burning question of what European women thought

of the erotic statuary found at
some of the temples. She described
Allahabad's Akshai Bar temple,
reached by way of a dimly lit set of
dirty stairs: "Our guide . . . led us
along dark passages, and did the
honours of various disgusting
idols, stuck in niches, some as large
as life, others quite small, but all
alike hideous, and all adorned with
flowers, and wet with the libations
of the holy Ganges water . . . [Y]ou
could not enter without a shuddering impression of earthly and
sensual devil-worship." After some
months had passed, she confessed,
"There is something startling in

Constance Gordon
Cumming. Gordon Cumming,
Wanderings in China, Edinburgh:
Blackwood, 1888, frontispiece.

the rapidity with which one gets quite at home
amongst all this paraphernalia of heathenism . . .
Now," she added, "we quite forgot to be shocked. It
was all so natural and seemed so entirely in accor-
dance with the feeling of the people!"[14]

At Simla, Gordon Cumming hooked up with a Captain and
Mrs. Graves for a three-month trek to the Tibetan frontier. They
passed through incredible mountain terrain generally following
the Sutlej River and came upon tiny terraced fields of white poppies. She was carried by bearers while "Mrs. Graves, being a
first-rate walker . . . walked every step of the way, occasionally
diverging down some frightful native path, or over some tremendous hill-top, whence she returned a few hours later to make me
envious by descriptions of spots to me unattainable."[15]

In a cholera-infested area she fell so ill—not from the deadly
disease but from bad potatoes—that she thought she'd sleep eter-
nally among the Himalaya cedars. The symptoms were routed with
her much-depended-upon castor oil. The farthest point the group
reached was Rarung, where they were able to get a glimpse of
Tibet. (Rarung has not been located. Either many of the places
Gordon Cumming visited have disappeared, or her spelling rendered her route almost unfollowable.)

A dak gharry.
Knox Boy Travellers by Thomas W. Knox,
New York: Harper & Brothers, 1881, 419.

The Himalayas were also the goal of Marie de Ujfalvy-Bourdon, who accompanied her husband Karl Eugen von Ujfalvy on his anthropological studies in 1881.[16]

The newly installed railway made their trip from Bombay to Amballa, in the Punjab, a quick and painless process. They left on 14 May and arrived on the 12th, thanks to a typographical error in her article published in the *Tour du monde* (1883). They then proceeded to Simla by dak gharry. There the viceroy arranged permission for them to visit Srinagar, a trip apparently not regularly allowed at the time.

The couple's luggage, carried by twenty porters, consisted of a tent, furniture and utensils. In addition, they had servants and horses with keepers. The number of helpers alternately shrank and swelled along the route, as did the animals; at one point Marie adopted a gazelle, but it died en route. Also with them was a Mr. Clarke, who was on a collecting mission for the South Kensington Museum, now London's Science Museum. Their route took them across the Sutlej River, along mountain passes and through hamlets. Karl Eugen amassed anthropological data along the way, mostly measuring people's heads, an ordeal to which his subjects submitted at times willingly, at times in fear.

Marie de Ujfalvy-Bourdon in sensible Himalayan gear. G. Vuillier,
Tour du monde 46, 1883: 393.

Marie was often transported by *ton jon*, but for one excursion to a hilltop fortress, she was popped

Another Himalayas traveller, Nina Mazuchelli, author of The Indian Alps and How We Crossed Them *(1876), in a* ton jon. Reprinted in Knox Boy Travellers *by* Thomas W. Knox, New York: Harper & Brothers, 1881, 422.

into a *dandy,* a portable hammock. Her porters charged up the steepest, shortest route, jumping from rock to rock like mountain goats, without taking her awkward situation into account. At the first stop she abandoned the contraption, and her porters pushed and pulled her up the rest of the way. The descent was made in a thunderstorm, not helped by the coming of night. She got back into her *dandy*—imagine the thing filling up like a bathtub with her sloshing about inside it—when, at an especially perilous moment, a gust of wind blew her and the men to the edge of a cliff. Somehow they made it down to the village.[17]

Their onward route took them through tea plantations and districts raging with cholera. Illness struck the entire party, and the rainy season was by now in full swing. The good care they were given by an English doctor did not stop Marie from complaining about his excessive fees.

At Srinagar, they met the maharajah of Kashmir and marvelled at the city's wealth. Gold, fine cloth and fruit were abundant, and the gardens, set amid the city's canals, were especially beautiful. They left in mid-August along mountainous terrain to the Baltistan town of Skardu, then continued north to their farthest destination, Askole, in the Karakoram range.

The route through the Karakorams was too difficult on horseback or in a *dandy,* so they walked. Marie remarked wryly, as she noticed how torn her boots were, that shoemakers would have rejoiced if all paths were as hard on footwear.[18] The couple turned back with regret, knowing how close they were to Tibet, but it was now September and the mountains would soon become impassable. After a few days in Srinagar and a side trip to Shalimar (near Lahore) to see the famous gardens, they left for Rawalpindi, where they caught a train back to Bombay.

Shalimar's gardens were immortalized by Laurence Hope, in a collection of bewitching poems about India called *Garden of Kama* (1901). Hope was in fact Adela Florence Cory, a young woman ruled by passion rather than by propriety and, like Isabelle

Eberhardt, ill at ease in the world she was born into. In 1881, at the age of sixteen, having finished her schooling, she left England and went to India to be with her parents. Already well travelled and independent, she was a somewhat unorthodox addition to Anglo society in Lahore, where she helped her father edit his military newspaper. In 1889, she met the love of her life, handsome and flamboyant Malcolm Nicolson, a colonel in the Bengal Army who was almost twice her age. They married, and she accompanied him to the remote northwest frontier, at times dressed as a Pathan boy in order to do so. Even when she was back in the structured society she loathed, she couldn't conform and wore her hair loose and received visitors in bare feet.

Laurence Hope (Adela Florence Cory). Selected Poems from the Indian Love Lyrics of Laurence Hope, London: William Heinemann, 1922, frontispiece.

Her writing expressed a deep love for her adventurous and gloriously free life. Legend has it that she became the mistress of an Indian prince, and her poem "On the City Wall" could be literally interpreted as proof of such an affair. However, two months after Nicolson's death in 1904, she committed suicide.[19]

Of the thousands of European women who lived and travelled in India, many left diaries, letters and books. Those who stand out resisted the safety of structured Anglo-Indian life and sought to understand the country on its own terms. When they succeeded they were amply rewarded with insights into a rich and cultured land.

Oceania
The Round-the-Worlders Converge

To someone from the northern hemisphere, Oceania, as a geographical designation, has the feel of a bottom drawer in which odds and ends are tossed. Made up of the many islands of the South Pacific, Southeast Asia, plus Australia, Tasmania and New Zealand, the region is unnervingly diverse, and few were the travellers who managed to explore it all.

AUSTRALIA and TASMANIA

Probably the first account of Australia to be published by a woman was *Voyage Round the World* (1795) by Mary Ann Parker, the English wife of John Parker, captain of the man-of-war *Gorgon*. Her voyage took her to the Cape, Australia and Norfolk Island and back to England.

Parker was happy at home; she had two children and was close to her mother, with whom she had travelled to France, Italy and Spain, but when her husband proposed this journey and gave her two weeks to make up her mind, it took her less than a minute to decide.

The journey out was tolerable. Only two of the crew died; she had a "suitable companion," in the person of Mrs. King, the wife of the governor of Norfolk; and, as she spoke Spanish, she acted as "Interpreter General" when they anchored at Spanish-speaking ports.[1]

They arrived at Port Jackson (north of Sydney) in September 1791. She toured Sydney Cove and Paramatta, noted the decent prospects for settlers and commented on the heavy cost of maintaining the colony and the shocking state of undress of "the Inhabitants of New South Wales, both male and female." She also tried some of the local cuisine; "I have often ate part of a kingaroo [*sic*]," she wrote, "with as much glee as if I had been a partaker of some of the greatest delicacies . . . although latterly I was cloyed with them, and found them very disagreeable."[2]

"A Cavalcade of Hawaiian Women." Isabella Bird learned to ride astride from horse-women such as these when she was in the Sandwich Islands (Hawaii). Émile Bayard, Tour du monde 26, 1873: 217.

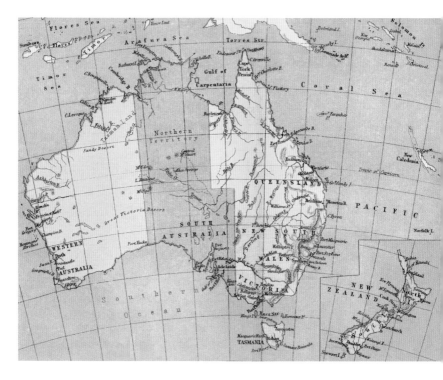

Australia, Tasmania and New Zealand.

Philips' Handy Atlas, c. 1897.

For the return journey, the ship, which had been filled with men, livestock and provisions, was loaded up with kangaroos, opposums "and every curiosity which that country produced."[3] They left in December; Captain Parker died of yellow fever somewhere along the way, and she disembarked a widow.

Louisa Anne Meredith, author of *Notes and Sketches of New South Wales* (1844), also accompanied her husband to Australia. Unlike Parker, however, Meredith was planning to stay. Her husband, who had established himself in Australia before they were married, was bringing her out to live with him. The couple left England in June 1839 on the *Letitia,* a merchant ship bound for Sydney non-stop. Her hopes for visiting Madeira and Tenerife dashed, she concentrated on making the most of shipboard life, though sea-sickness dampened the first few weeks. Her account is a lively and sympathetic rendering of life on a cramped sailing vessel.

Shortly after arriving, she and her husband travelled to Bathurst, some 190 kilometres from the capital. Her portrayals of plants, insects and scenery are well executed, as are her pithy observations of the living conditions of Aborigines and the status of social-climbing ex-convicts, but she excels at describing the dismal state of New South Wales hostelries. The Merediths put up at numerous inns, one of which was called the Rivulet. With newly painted walls, this hotel promised high style; alas, it was a scene of "bacchanalian orgies" and worse. Upon inspection of their room, Meredith found sheets so black that "half a dozen unwashed chimney-sweeps occupying the same bed for a fortnight could not have left evidences of a darker hue." After much grumbling, the hostess gave her a set of cleaner ones. Meredith remade the beds and was getting ready to retire when the maid knocked. "If you please, ma'am," she said, "Missus wants them sheets you pulled off your bed, for a gentleman as is just come in!" Using her parasol, Meredith pushed the filthy things out the door.[4]

An English reviewer praised Meredith's book, writing, "It is a real pleasure to accompany such a lady over sea and land—though the former stretched monotonously around her during a four-months' merchant-vessel passage—and was exchanged for the scorched 'ever-brown' surface of a country devoid of any past or present interest, whether of an historical, poetical, pictorial, or social kind—New South Wales."[5]

Meredith also lived in Tasmania and Victoria and wrote other books, including *My Home in Tasmania during a Residence of Nine Years* (1852), *Our Island Home* (1879) and *Tasmanian Friends and Foes: Feather, Furred and Finned* (1880). She died in Melbourne in 1895.

Ellen Clacy, an unmarried, high-spirited English girl with a now-lost maiden name, went to Australia with her brother in 1852, inspired by reports of the great wealth to be found at the "Diggings." She returned to England less than a year later, towing a Mr. Charles Clacy and planning a book: *A Lady's Visit to the Gold Diggings of Australia* (1853).

From Melbourne, brother and sister headed out to the gold fields of Bendigo, but not before she could say a word or two about the rough-living, big-spending capital of Victoria. Prices were sky high, tempting new arrivals to sell the clothes off their backs for handsome profits. According to Clacy, everything was second-rate; the sherry

The buckboard, a common means of travel in Australia. Brassey 1889, 280.

was trash, the omnibus simple wagons, the houses wretched. Hotels were crammed beyond capacity, so their party, which had swelled to six, wound up in a private home, the five lads jammed into one room and Clacy sharing a bed with the lady of the house. The Melbourne nights were filled with the sounds of dogs barking and revolvers firing.

So great was their excitement at their prospects for striking it rich, however, that none of these discomforts, or the threat of robbers or pouring rain, could dampen their fever. At Bendigo they staked their claims; Clacy kept house (or rather, tent) and panned, while the men dug. Her descriptions of the voyage and of Melbourne are amusing, but her account of the gold fields is fascinating. From the thousands of people "digging, wheeling, carrying, and washing," to a young orphan girl alone in her tent with the body of her dead grandfather, Clacy let little pass by without succinct comment. Of herself we know little, except that she was a "pocket edition of the feminine sex" and that she was incapacitated by fear during a holdup.[6] Clacy followed up *A Lady's Visit* with novels.

Sisters Florence and Rosamond Hill, authors of *What We Saw in Australia* (1875), took their interest in good works with them to

Australia and made much of the fact that they were heading off unescorted. They dismissed the adventure, saying that it was now easy to travel to the Antipodes, yet when friends heard that the two were going alone, they thought the women were crazy. The Hills were right; their trip wasn't a big deal. Early in 1873, they travelled to Venice by rail to catch a comfortable P&O steamship; their stay in Egypt was made easier with the help of a cousin. At Adelaide, an aunt let them use her home as a base for nearly six months.

What makes the Hills' trip interesting is their choice of tourist activities. They tolerated a few mountains and lakes, but their goal was to visit as many prisons, orphanages, reformatories, farms, mines and paupers' asylums as possible. The highlight of Sydney was their visit of the harbour, where they took in the reform school housed on a boat and an industrial school on Cockatoo Island.[7] What would these two good sisters have said if they knew that Petty's, their hotel in Sydney, had housed the immoral Lola Montez twenty years earlier?

The Hills' philanthropic concerns were so relentless and their book so earnest that they must have put tourism in Australia back by a decade.

The SOUTH PACIFIC and SOUTHEAST ASIA

Whereas Australia was rough and tumble, the South Pacific and Southeast Asia was distant, wild and malarial. Travellers to the area either had a vocation, such as a husband or a job, or were the rare brave sort like Ida Pfeiffer, who went twice. Her first trip was in December 1846, when she caught a Dutch barque from Valparaiso to Hong Kong via Tahiti, one stage of her first journey around the world. Tahiti confounded her; it was a paradise, but she couldn't accept the "depraved" lives of the pleasure-loving Tahitians. Their sinful relationships with the European sailors who regularly landed there were especially upsetting. But they were hospitable to her, and

The Braganza, *taken by Ida Pfeiffer in 1847, from Singapore to Ceylon. It was originally destined for the London-Constantinople route. ILN, 6 July 1844: 4.*

her three-week stay was amply rewarded by the beauty of the island and the abundance of strange and delightful fruit and shellfish.

Pfeiffer's second trip to Oceania, at the age of fifty-four, was part of her second journey around the world. She left Vienna in March 1851, partially financed by a £150 grant by the Austrian government and partly through discounts or free rides she was given on account of her near-celebrity status as a writer. The Asian portion of her route took her to what was then known as the Eastern Archipelago (Indonesia): Singapore, Borneo, Java, Sumatra, the Celebes, Ceram and the Moluccas. In Borneo, she was comfortably lodged at the home of Rajah James Brooke, but after a short stay, she plunged into the jungle, where she had the thrill of seeing two newly severed human heads, the result of a current Dayak tribal war.

Through Brooke's efforts, Borneo had been somewhat tamed, but Sumatra, her next stop, had no such disciplinarian and reports of Battacker tribesmen murdering Europeans were common. Undaunted, Pfeiffer covered some 1100 kilometres on horseback and 240 on foot, eased her way out of a confrontation with cannibals and shared native huts, including one with a murderer who seemed to be in the last stages of tuberculosis. The hardships she withstood from these expeditions took their toll, and in spite of what she called her "almost indestructible constitution," she began to suffer from malarial fever.[8]

Her presence in Borneo and Sumatra was "a very new and surprising phenomenon. Very few [natives]

Ida Pfeiffer was apparently short, frail and a bit hunched, but she walked extremely quickly for her age. Whenever she returned from travelling, she sported a deep tan; her features otherwise revealed none of her extraordinary experiences. Mettais, after a photo, Tour du monde 5, 1862: 405.

had ever seen a white man, and none a white woman; and their astonishment was so much the greater, since, according to their ideas, a woman alone can hardly venture more than a few yards from her hut." She attributed her ability to travel with relative ease to her sex. "Had I been a man," she wrote of Sumatra, "they would have taken me for a spy, and either sent me back, or, what is more likely, put me to death."[10]

As an author, she was flattered when the king of the Celebes, who had heard that she was writing a book, offered her "100 rupees for a copy in his own language. What a gallant King!" she exclaimed. "What might I not have done, and how might the plan of my travels have been extended, if I could only have induced people in Europe to think as much of me!"[11]

Most travellers left Southeast Asia for their health; Anna Leonowens *went* to Singapore with her husband for that reason. When he died, she taught to support herself and her two children. Her life was turned upside down after she received a letter from the king of Siam in February 1862, asking her to come and teach his children. Although the job did not immediately appeal to her, Leonowens decided to take a chance. With her young son, Louis, in tow, she caught the steamer *Chow Phya* from Singapore to Paknam (Samut Prakan) near Bangkok.

Her first views of Siam took her breath away:

Here were the strange floating city, with its stranger people on all the open porches, quays, and jetties; the innumerable rafts and boats, canoes and gondolas, junks, and ships; the pall of black smoke from the steamer, the burly roar of the engine, and the murmur and the jar; the bewildering cries of men, women, and children, the shouting of the Chinamen, and the barking of the dogs,—yet no one seemed troubled but me.[12]

Nothing had been arranged for her, so she spent the first night at the house of a compatriot, Captain B——. The next day, the prime minister installed her in his own palace, where she became the centre of attention of his harem. The women asked her if she would prefer to become the wife of the premier or of the king. When she replied that she'd rather be put to a slow death than marry either, they were amazed, as it meant passing up a ransom's worth of jewels and gold.[13]

Paknam; what would have been Anna Leonowens first view of Siam.
Sabatier, Tour du monde 8, 1863: 222.

She was finally taken to meet the king, and her description of the entry to the Imperial Palace is truly out of a fairy tale. Escorted by Captain B——, she walked along a covered path that passed several temples. One housed the massive gold-plated "Sleeping Idol." Another, the Temple of the Emerald Idol, was adorned with emblems, mythological figures and constellations. The altar, a 30-metre-high pyramid, was topped by a golden spire, and the floor was paved with polished brass. The Emerald Idol itself was made of gold and encrusted with precious stones.

They climbed the marble stairs and walked unannounced into a grand hall. Leonowens wrote, "Ranged on the carpet were many prostrate, mute, and motionless forms, over whose heads to step was a temptation as drolly natural as it was dangerous. His Majesty spied us quickly, and advanced abruptly, petulantly screaming, 'Who? who? who?'" Captain B—— had warned her to expect a battery of personal questions. The king fired off the first: "How old

The king of Siam, Somdetch P'hra Paramendr Maha Mongkut, and his wife.
E. Bocourt, after a photo, *Tour du monde* 8, 1863: 225.

shall you be?" to which she replied, "One hundred and fifty years old." She continued:

Had I made myself much younger, he might have ridiculed or assailed me; but now he stood surprised and embarrassed for a few moments ... and at last, beginning to perceive the jest, coughed, laughed, coughed again, and in a high sharp key asked, "In what year were you borned?

Instantly I struck a mental balance, and answered, as gravely as I could, "In 1788."

At this point the expression of his Majesty's face was indescribably comical. Captain B—— slipped behind a pillar to laugh ... His Majesty ... returned to the attack with *élan*.

"How many years shall you be married?"

"For several years, your Majesty."

He fell into a brown study; then, laughing, rushed at me, and demanded triumphantly:—

"Ha! How many grandchildren shall you now have? Ha, ha! How many! How many! Ha, ha, ha!"[14]

Leonowens's six years at court were spent humouring and defying the king. Her classes swelled to include not only the king's many offspring but his wives as well. She also became a translator, lobbyist and diplomat. Her health gave out in the summer of 1866, and she departed a year later. Although she was exhausted with life in the "tumultuous East," she found the parting difficult and left in tears. The king told her that everyone would miss her, even though she was a "difficult woman, and more difficult than generality."[15] Her story was made into a hugely successful stage play and two films.

Isabella Bird undertook her journey to the Antipodes—begun midway through 1872—on account of poor health. For her, insomnia, nerves and a bad back were good reasons for leaving her home and her frail sister, Henrietta, and travelling to Australia. But Australia did not impress her, so she decided to push on to the United States, which she had visited as a young woman. An

Isabella Bird.
ILN, 27 June 1891: 839.

unplanned stop at the Sandwich Islands (Hawaii) en route, to help nurse an ailing fellow passenger, turned into a six-month stay. Captivated by the wild and lush terrain, she explored it all astride a horse, in spite of her severely pained spine. In fact, her health was restored to an astonishing degree. In sunshine and in heavy rains, crossing torrential rivers and deep valleys, she rode to such places as the active volcanoes of Kilauea and Mauna Loa. She often stayed at the homes of hospitable Hawaiians, as there were few inns. She usually offered a small payment, but at Waipio the host refused money, saying that "he should be ashamed of himself if he took anything from a lady travelling without a husband."[16] She also visited missionaries, as she did on all her future journeys; she maintained an unfailing interest in the good works of the church. *The Hawaiian Archipelago: Six Months among the Palm Groves, Coral*

Reefs and Volcanoes of the Sandwich Islands (1875) resulted from this trip.

Six years later, she was in Southeast Asia, after touring the interior of Japan. In January 1878, she headed to Saigon and Singapore and from there to Malacca, where she was to explore what is now Malaysia for six weeks. The resulting book was *The Golden Chersonese and the Way Thither* (1883). Through the efforts of her contacts, Bird enjoyed the hospitality, the law and order and the beautiful climate and scenery. Without the hardships that marked her other journeys, she had the leisure to fill in details about flora and fauna and statistics on people and the economy.

For this reader, the highlight of the book came during her stay at the British Residency at Kwala Kangsa, in the state of Perak. In the absence of the resident, Mr. Low, she was welcomed by his servant. Travel worn, unable to change her clothes and in no mood for company, she made her way to the dining room, where the table was set for three. After she sat down, the other guests were led in by two servants. They were Mahmoud and Eblis, two charming but unpredictable apes. The dinner, a true tropical fantasy, proceeded in a stately fashion, only occasionally disrupted by Mahmoud's energetic grabbing for the dishes as they passed by. Bird asked, "Shall I ever enjoy a dinner party so much again?"[17]

Emily Innes, a magistrate's wife, took exception to Bird's glowing assessment of Malaysia and wrote her own take on the gruesomeness of life for European women there, *The Chersonese With the Gilding Off* (1885). Innes had good reason to complain. She had been staying at the home of the Lloyds when Captain Lloyd was murdered and Mrs. Lloyd's skull fractured, apparently by a Chinese gang. Innes herself was also knocked about. Bird alluded to the incident but gave it and other aggravations only a few pages.[18]

Marianne North, another world traveller, made two trips to Oceania. The first was in 1876 on her first round-the-world—but by no means her first long-distance—journey. She stayed with the Brookes at Sarawak (Kuching) and then went to Java. From there she continued on to Ceylon and finally back to England.

Four years later, she was persuaded by Mrs. Brooke to return with her and the rajah to Sarawak. North spent six weeks painting, botanizing and trekking through the jungle, then went on to

Australia—her first stop, Brisbane. For the next six months, she zipped around Australia, mostly in coaches, sometimes alone, sometimes with a female companion. The coach line, Cobbe and Co., was so proud to be carrying unaccompanied ladies that it "telegraphed beforehand to all the halting-places to have an extra quantity of beef ready."[19]

Melbourne, North declared, was "by far the most real city in Australia."[20] She also went to Adelaide, then on to Perth by sea. She returned to Melbourne, then visited Tasmania, New Zealand and Hawaii. North's travels, undertaken mostly as part of her program to paint and collect rare plants, though unusual and demanding, lacked Pfeiffer's daring. As well, North was better connected and better funded.

Marianne North travelled extensively through Southeast Asia, the Eastern Archipelago and Australia in search of new and exotic plants to paint. A number of plants were named after her, including Northea seychellana, Nepenthes northiana, Crinum northianum, Areca northiana and Kniphofia northiae.[21]

Photo by Elliot and Fry, North 1893, frontispiece.

Constance Gordon Cumming, who also had means, landed in the South Pacific as a companion to the new governor of Fiji's wife. When she was given the chance to tour on a man-of-war, she couldn't resist. From her travels in the region in the 1870s, she wrote three books: *At Home in Fiji* (1881), *A Lady's Cruise in a French Man-of-War* (1882) and *Fire Fountains of the Sandwich Isles* (1883).

Anna Forbes travelled around the Eastern Archipelago in the mid-1880s with her husband, naturalist Henry O. Forbes. She marvelled at the architecture, climate and tropical vegetation; even the European guests at the Hotel der Nederlanden in Batavia (Djakarta) were remarkable in what was to her their perpetual state of *déshabillé*. She was shocked that Dutch women wore their hair loose, sported sarongs and stuffed their stockingless feet into slippers, but she was eventually convinced to wear such an outfit herself. *Insulinde: Experiences of a Naturalist's Wife in the*

The Brasseys fording a stream in Borneo.
Brassey 1889, facing p. 196.

Eastern Archipelago (1887) reveals how small Anna's world had been and shows her willingness to participate in this new life and to adapt, even if slowly, to new ways.

The Forbeses explored the Dutch East Indies thoroughly in the interests of Henry's studies. The trip was often difficult, and the trying conditions prompted a young Portuguese woman, whom Forbes had met briefly, to admit that it had been her dream to be the wife of an explorer, but she could now see that it wasn't all "romance and perpetual picknicking."[22]

The couple visited Surabaja, Macassar (where she couldn't find a trace of the famed hair oil), New Guinea, the islands of Banda, Amboina and, their real goal, Timor Laut (Tanimbar Islands), where Henry left her to go into the interior. It was at this last stop that she succumbed to fear and fever. On one occasion, she set off to the port, hoping to get her letters on the next steamer, but she was so terrified of meeting man or beast that she took the wrong route and broke down and cried when she had to share the path with a lone native. As well, thieves took everything portable from her house, and she was unable to keep herself supplied with food. Exacerbated by her isolation, the malaria, which had been occasionally plaguing her, nearly got the better of her, and she wrote that if it hadn't been for the vision of Henry finding her dead body gnawed by rats, which became more insolent by the day, she would have let herself die. She managed to get a message to the doctor in the next village and was rescued. Henry hastened back, and the couple agreed she had to return to England.

That Anna was not prepared mentally or physically for such a trip is clear; her helplessness was tragic. She concluded that difficult living conditions eliminated the Dutch East Indies as a potential tourist destination. This pronouncement did not stop Lady Annie Brassey and her family from landing there in 1887 in their yacht, the *Sunbeam,* on what turned out to be her last voyage. She was the mother of five children, the author of five very popular, beautifully produced books about her travels and an enthusiastic collector of natural history specimens. Her husband, Thomas, was an MP, and she tirelessly campaigned for him; yet the pair managed to wangle long stretches of time away from political and household duties and wander at will. They had already visited the Arctic, the Caribbean, South America and Polynesia in the *Sunbeam,* a 540-tonne, three-masted schooner that carried about forty crew and passengers. This voyage, begun in November 1886, took them through the Mediterranean, through the Red Sea to Aden, then to Bombay, Ceylon, Rangoon, Singapore, Borneo, Sarawak, Macassar, West Australia, Adelaide, Melbourne and Sydney, and back across the Indian Ocean. Lady Annie's burial at sea on 14 September 1887 at 15°50′ S, 110°38′ E, was noted only by a poignant black cross in the ship's log, appended to her book *The Last Voyage, 1886–1887* (1889). Her account was finished by her husband and a close friend.

Lady Annie Brassey.
ILN, 22 October 1887: 483.

Lady Annie had hinted in her other books that she wasn't at the peak of health. It's a miracle that more lady travellers did not meet their ends during their adventures, for no matter how wealthy they were, even minor illness and accidents in the nineteenth century could become disasters, not just inconveniences.

Staying Alive

CRISTINA DI BELGIOJOSO DEVELOPED ONE IN ALEPPO. Ida Pfeiffer had been warned of them and prematurely congratulated herself for emerging from Mesopotamia with only a superficial one, but when she got home a mass of them erupted and plagued her for eight months. Anne Blunt was scared stiff of them but managed to escape them altogether. Were they bug bites? No, they were Aleppo buttons, ugly boils that could deeply scar their victims. These ghastly things, also known as Nile buttons, Baghdad boils and Date marks—now known to be caused by parasites—were encountered in Egypt, Syria and Iraq. Belgiojoso's was nothing compared with the thirteen buttons that adorned the nose of a Polish colonel she met.[1]

Boils were an irritation; malaria, ague, plague, cholera and yellow fever could kill. Governments responded to germ-carrying travellers by instituting quarantines, especially for those arriving by sea. Women wrote of being imprisoned on their ships or in quarantine houses, or *lazarettos,* often squalid, ill-furnished sheds into which too many people were crammed.

Yesterday's women travellers would have scoffed at modern-day women who are reluctant to travel because of pregnancy. Anne Blunt didn't let pregnancies or at least two miscarriages—one in Algeria, one in Arabia (not to mention several in Europe)—stop her from getting on with her journeys. Neither did Lady Londonderry, who miscarried in Vienna. Ann Fanshawe, according to different sources, had fourteen, seventeen or eighteen babies, roughly the same number as the number of journeys she made.

Add to disease and pregnancy the generally fragile and susceptible states that many women admitted themselves to be in, and one wonders how they were able to travel at all.

᠁"On account of the many extraordinary stories related to me of the Aleppo Button (boil), I had some curiosity to see and judge for myself what there was true in them . . . Twenty-four hours passed in Aleppo, convinced me of the universality of this malady."—Cristina di Belgiojoso[2]

Ship passengers who had already spent months on board could look forward to further delays from quarantine officers. This ship was docked at a West Indian port. Harper's Weekly, 29 November 1873: 1069.

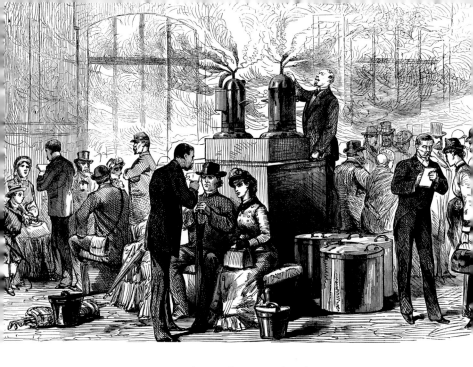

Those who wanted to keep healthy had an assortment of tricks, ranging from wearing flannel around the middle in hot climates to ward off chills and taking quinine or smoking tobacco in malarial regions. Drinking wine was widespread, especially in the eighteenth century, because of poisonous water. Dysentery and cholera, ailments that attacked the intestinal tract, were common and usually dealt with by taking opium to control the resulting diarrhoea. During a period of famine and flood in southern India, Marianne North wrote, "Every one was taking opium, so I followed the fashion, prevention being better than cure." In Yokohama, she developed such a severe case of rheumatism that she sent for an American doctor. "[He] injected morphia into my arm, and put me to sleep for twenty-four hours. The people in the hotel thought I was dead."[3]

As far as I can find, women travellers generally did not drink or take drugs recreationally, though there were exceptions. Sailing in the *Canada* from Liverpool to Halifax in 1854, Isabella Bird was disgusted with her constantly tipsy cabin mate, who kept a supply of gin, brandy and beer tucked in her berth. Cristina di Belgiojoso experimented with hashish in Damascus but was disappointed with it. "I smoked hashish, I ate it, I drank it, but all in vain. My brain (I will not say my mind) being exempt from vertigo, I remained almost impassible."[4] Belgiojoso also grew opium poppies on her farm in Turkey. Isabelle Eberhardt was well known for her kif smoking and absinthe drinking. With her they became habits that threatened her already precarious health.

Lady Mary Duffus Hardy fought tooth and nail to get a gentleman to escort her to an opium den in San Francisco's Chinatown. Bird had a ready-made one on her houseboat on the Yangtze but declined its pleasures. As it was, the fumes mixing with her darkroom chemicals and the insalubrious mists from the river must have turned her head a few times.

Fanny Parks discoursed on the use of ganja, bhang, datura and arrack in India and tried opium first-hand, when she took a large hunk of it to ease a pain in her face. Under its influence, she became blissfully happy and even more talkative than usual until the next morning, when she needed treatment for a headache caused by the opium. Of a delicacy of sautéed poppy heads she remarked, "If you only eat enough, you will become as tipsy as mortal may desire."[5]

Numerous women who travelled to or lived in the East smoked tobacco. Burton thought women could gracefully smoke cigarettes, narghilehs or chibouques but disapproved of cigars and clay pipes. Belgiojoso smoked a narghileh even before heading to Turkey. The chibouque, a long-stemmed pipe, was Harriet Martineau's choice; she said, "I saw no more reason why I should not take it than why English ladies should not take their daily glass of sherry at home—an indulgence which I do not need." Martineau could easily dispense with a regular tipple; she relied on mesmerism and opium to get her through her days.[6]

A narghileh-smoking Algerian woman. Postcard, c. 1900.

China, Japan & Tibet
Faith & Folly

IN JULY 1847, a European woman carrying a worn carpetbag stepped off a junk at the busy port of Canton. She and the boat's captain walked through the maze of streets in search of the house of a Mr. Agassiz, for whom she had a letter of introduction. With the captain's help, she found the address, bade him goodbye and knocked on the door. Mr. Agassiz' reaction on seeing diminutive fifty-year-old Ida Pfeiffer standing there by herself was alarm, then astonishment. Pfeiffer later wrote that he could "hardly credit that I had met with no difficulties or injury. From him I learned what risks I, as a woman, had run in traversing the streets of Canton with no escort but a Chinese guide. Such a thing had never occurred before."[1]

It had been only five years—since the signing of the Treaty of Nanking—that non-Asian women were allowed into any of China's five treaty ports, of which Canton (Guangzhou) was one. And even now they were barely tolerated. Did Pfeiffer not know any better? Was she not aware that for over a hundred years, Europeans in Canton had been controlled by eight strict rules, one of which was *no women?*[2] That these rules had been dismantled by the 1842 treaty made little difference; there were still few foreign women in the city.

But she must have heard about Anne Noble, who had been shipwrecked off Hangzhou in 1841, losing her husband and baby in the tragedy. After receiving kind attention from the locals, the survivors were seized by soldiers, and Noble, dressed in rags, was marched to prison in chains. To her further shame, she was stuck in a small cage and moved from town to town. She was eventually released.

Fortunately, Pfeiffer's five weeks in Canton passed without incident, though the threat of violence was always in the air. Her only concession to the restrictions on women, aside from securing a male escort to accompany her on her forays through the city, was to wear

Catherine de Bourboulon dressed for travel. Émile Bayard, Tour du monde 11, 1865: 241.

China and Japan. Philips' Handy Atlas, c. 1897.

male attire on a tour of the walls. Pfeiffer mentioned one other European woman, a Mrs. Balt, the wife of a missionary, and observed that the few traders who brought their families let them out only in closed litters.[3] Constance Gordon Cumming, Annie Brassey and Isabella Bird were to come to Canton in the 1870s, but by then women could move about freely.

The four other ports open to Europeans were Shanghai, Amoy (Xiamen), Ningpo (Ningbo) and Foochow (Fuzhou). Thirty-two-year-old Catherine MacLeod de Bourboulon lived in Shanghai in 1859, at the end of the second Opium War. Scottish by birth, she was married to a French diplomat, who was in China from 1859 to 1862 to negotiate France's share of the Treaty of Tientsin. It was an extraordinary time for any westerner to witness, let alone a woman. Embroiled in the Taiping Revolution, China was the scene of starvation, massacre and torture, much of it visible from Bourboulon's apartment. In November 1860, she and her husband left for Tientsin and its newly established French legation.

In March 1861, they moved to Peking (Beijing), where they saw more evidence of atrocities, though the city was relatively safe for Europeans. Extracts from her diary, published in the *Tour du monde* (1864–65), were illustrated with gruesome beheadings and laterally bisected bodies, as well as with scenes of everyday life, proof that a semblance of normalcy was being maintained during the

Bourboulon's camp at Homoutch. Émile Bayard, *Tour du monde* 11, 1865: 233.

revolution. The first part of her account deals with life in Shanghai; the second half, which is of interest to us here, with her crossing from Peking to Moscow.

In spite of her sufferings from an unspecified malady, the couple decided to return to Paris in 1862 by land, having already made the trip by sea five times. They knew it could be done; Mme de Baluseck, the wife of the Russian minister, had already come overland from Moscow and would return there with them. The party also included English ambassador Sir Frederick Bruce, who would turn back before the frontier. In addition to two supply caravans sent out in advance and laden with such essentials as champagne, there were a dozen light carriages, two palanquins (one for Bourboulon when she tired of riding and the other for her puppies), horses, mules, camels, servants (Bruce brought his own maître d'hôtel), guides, escorts, an interpreter and a doctor. With permission to cross China's borders, the party set off in May on a four-month journey of approximately twelve thousand kilometres.

Their route took them northwest to the Great Wall, through the Gobi Desert to Ourga (Ulan Bator), Verkhneudkinsk (Ulan-Ude) and Irkutsk, then west to Krasnoyarsk, Omsk, Ekaterinburg (Sverdlovsk) and Moscow, over mountains, through deserts and past magnificent temples and tombs. Even though many of the habitations they passed through consisted only of a cluster of small huts, huge crowds turned out to see them.

At the beginning, the travellers stayed at inns; as they progressed, however, they camped in tents expressly built for them. After a distressing night in a stinking, dirty inn, Bourboulon wrote that tents were a "thousand times better." And no wonder. Theirs had a diameter of about five metres and a height of three, and were sumptuously outfitted with wooden doors, silk hangings and carpets.[4]

Lest the journey seem too luxurious, it's only fair to point out that they were frequently overcome by dust storms, vehicles broke down and the continuous jarring motion, whether on horseback or palanquin, was a painful trial for Bourboulon. "It's only with the force of energy," she wrote, "that I can support the fatigue of each day. If I let myself be discouraged, how could I reach the Siberian frontier still two hundred leagues away? It's certainly sad to be gravely ill in these deserts." That said, it's worthwhile noting that she and her party were probably the first to play whist in the Gobi desert.[5]

Bourboulon's health improved as they crossed Siberia to Ekaterinburg. The rest of the trip, to Moscow and on to Paris, was made by steamer and train. She died three years later. In the 1865 *Handbook for Travellers to Russia, Poland and Finland,* Murray's remarked that "many travellers of both sexes have already performed the overland journey . . . and reported favourably on the facility with which it may be accomplished notwithstanding even a complete ignorance of the Russian language." They suggested allowing fifty days from London to Peking.[6]

Isabella Bird's sketch of herself in a Japanese "straw rain-cloak."

Bird 1880, vol. 1, 346.

Isabella Bird's extensive travels through Asia were most often made with only an interpreter and, at times, porters, for company. In this fashion, she toured Japan and Korea, sailed up the Yangtze and attempted to reach Tibet.

Bird arrived in Japan after a four-year hiatus from travelling. Following her trip to the Sandwich Islands and the United States, she had returned home to her sister Henrietta in 1874 and resumed her invalid ways. In 1878, she received a proposal of marriage from an old friend, Dr. John Bishop, who, like Isabella and Henrietta, was chronically ill. Rather than consider

such a future, she left for Asia, once again for her "health," starting in Japan and ending in Malaysia. Advice, both at home and in Japan, was not auspicious. Bird wrote, "As no English lady has yet travelled alone through the interior, my project excites a very friendly interest . . . and I receive much warning and dissuasion, and little encouragement."[7]

ABOVE: *A European woman is transported in a palanquin through the streets of Shanghai.* E. Grandsire, *L'Illustration*, 13 October 1860: 261.

She made a seven-month journey into the interior and to Yezo (Hokkaido), accompanied by her youthful interpreter, Ito, and a passport allowing her unrestricted travel in the north. She travelled mostly

BELOW: *A* karuma, *a cart used by Bird to get around Tokyo.* Bird 1880, vol. 1, 85.

on horseback, during a season of unparalleled rain, along muddy paths through tiny villages to damp, squalid travellers' huts where she discovered that privacy was not a universal concept as curious villagers tore spy holes in the shoji screens that served as her walls. Her *Unbeaten Tracks in Japan* (1880) is a primer on psychological survival that today's authors of "bad trips" accounts can take lessons from.

On Christmas Eve 1878, Bird was heading for Hong Kong on the *Volga,* "a miserable steamer, with . . . nothing to sit on but the benches by the dinner-table in the dismal saloon. The master, a worthy man, so far as I ever saw of him, was Goth, Vandal, Hun, Visigoth, all in one."[8]

On New Year's Eve, she was on her way to Canton. The ss *Kin Kiang* carried two Europeans (one of whom was Bird) and 1950 Chinese. Bird spent ten days in Canton, freely touring the walls, exploring the narrow, busy streets, the hospitals, the floating city, even the overcrowded, indescribably filthy Naam-Hoi prison,

where the wretched inmates were fettered by heavy chains and the opium fumes choked the air. She was shaken by the atmosphere of cruelty and vice and by the execution grounds, which were "a field of blood."[9] From Canton she returned to Hong Kong, then went on to Malaysia.

When Henrietta died in 1880, Bird married Dr. Bishop and temporarily limited her travelling to Continental spas. Marianne North repeated a story about Bird that was circulating in 1881: "She was asked if she would not like to go to New Guinea. She said, 'Oh yes; but she was married now, and it was not the sort of place one could take a man to!'"[10] The two lived in mutual physical misery until Bishop's death in 1886. Three years later she was on her way to Kashmir and the Tibetan border, where she managed to reach the town of Leh in what was known as Little Tibet (Baltistan, now in Ladakh). She returned home via Persia.

Bird visited Korea and China from 1894 to 1897, and though Korea disappointed her, she was still able to write the two-volume *Korea and her Neighbours* (1898). China and the second attempt at

Tibet were far more challenging. Hostilities against foreigners were running high and travel was as appalling as in Japan and Persia. She packed lightly and wore a modified Chinese dress, which spoiled her for restrictive European clothing. She also took copious photographs, developing the film in makeshift darkrooms and rinsing out the hypo with silty Yangtze water. She sailed in houseboats scented by the fumes of the opium-smoking boatmen or was carried in a chair by bearers along muddy paths. Although her zest for travel had not diminished, her resulting book, *The Yangtze Valley and Beyond* (1899), had lost some of her earlier spirit. She was sixty-three and in worse health than ever, suffering from rheumatic gout, fatigue, a lung infection and heart degeneration.[11]

Bird made one last, six-month journey around Morocco in 1901, on horseback. Then, in 1902, shortly after being diagnosed with a tumour and heart disease, she prepared to return to China. That trip was never made; Isabella Bird died on 7 October 1904.[12]

A number of European woman attempted to reach Tibet. Charlotte Canning, vicereine of India, travelled to the India-Tibet border in 1860, as did Constance Gordon Cumming in the 1870s and Marie de Ujfalvy-Bourdon in 1883. Nina Mazuchelli, in the mid-1870s, Mrs. F. D. Bridges and Bird, in the late 1870s and 1889 respectively, made it to Leh in Little Tibet.

English missionary Annie Royle Taylor was the first European woman to cross into Tibet proper, in 1892, and was eventually allowed to live in Tibet. Traveller William Carey first met Taylor in July 1899, in her "shop" in the market town of Yatung (Yadong), north of Darjeeling. He had sought her out, hoping she could give him information about Tibetan customs for a book he was writing. It was during this visit that she gave him a glimpse of her nearly illegible diary. Carey left on his own travels but remained intrigued by her journal and eventually asked permission to transcribe it.[13]

As he painstakingly deciphered her scrawl, he discovered the story of a woman whose faith was so deep that she unwittingly risked her and her guides' lives on a mission to reach Lhasa to spread the word of God. She had been with the China Inland Mission since 1884, and after several years spent around the Tibetan border, she began planning her entry into that country.[14]

Annie Taylor outfitted for her trek into Tibet (left); Pontso, Annie Taylor and Pontso's unnamed mistress (right), drinking tea.
Carey, facing p. 198 and 242.

She left in September 1892, from the border town of Tau-chau★ along with her servants: Pontso, a Tibetan, who had come to China with her from India, and his mistress; Leucotze and Nobgey, Chinese men; and Noga, a Chinese guide, and his Tibetan wife, Erminie. They were almost immediately pitched headlong into a numbingly cold winter. And even though they joined a two-hundred-strong Mongol caravan, brigands relieved them of clothing and bedding. They were lucky not to have been killed. The ragged party staggered through snow and windstorms, halting as the Yellow River (Huang Ho) became too swollen to cross. To top it off, Noga began to beat his wife and threatened to turn Taylor over to Tibetan officials.

They eventually crossed the river on inflated animal skins, a gruelling feat that had to be done a second time when they encountered the winding river once again. By October, a less pious traveller would have given up. Taylor's stomach had rebelled

---

★ Tau-chau has been known as Tei-chu, Tai-chu, Tao-chow, and is possibly modern-day Luqu.

against the greasy Tibetan food, she fell ill from the glare of the sun off the snow, then Leucotze died. A month later Noga threatened to kill her. To her prayers she added the fervent wish that he would just leave, and he did in the middle of December. As a malicious final gesture, he informed on her, and on 4 January 1893, she was arrested on suspicion of spying. She was escorted to the town of Nag-chu-ka (Nagqu), a few days march from Lhasa, and summarily evicted from the country. The weary travellers headed back east to the border town of Ta-Chien-lu (Kangding) in Sichuan province. She wrote a pamphlet of her account—rather disappointing, according to Carey—called *The Origin of the Tibetan Pioneer Mission* (c. 1894). Other aspirants to Lhasa followed, but none were as poorly equipped as Taylor.

One of those hopefuls, Susie Carson Rijnhart, a doctor from Ontario, wrote *With the Tibetans in Tent and Temple* (1901) of her experience. She and her Dutch missionary husband, Petrus Rijnhart, went to China in the autumn of 1894 to set up a medical dispensary and Christian mission at Lusar, close to the Tibet border. From Lusar they moved to Tankar (Huangyuan), near the lamasery of Kumbum.[15] In the anticipation that they would get to Tibet, they tried to learn the language, though their teacher, it turned out, fed them a jumble of Mongolian and Tibetan; they did, however, become fluent in Chinese.

Shortly after their arrival, they were witness to a bloody Muslim rebellion. They were given the extraordinary privilege of sanctuary within the Lusar lamasery, and Susie's medical expertise, in demand from the start, was indispensable during the vicious fighting. On 30 June 1897, their son Charles was born; less than a year later, the couple was off to Lhasa.

Their planning seemed sensible enough; they organized a small, inconspicuous caravan with three men, including Rahmin, a Ladakh guide who had worked for the explorer Captain Wellby, along with five riding and twelve pack animals, and enough food to last two years. They left in mid-May 1898.

Although a horse immediately bolted and smashed a saddle, the expedition began smoothly enough. They crossed the Tsaidam plain in good weather, but as they ascended the Kunlun Shan Mountains, snow began to fall, and their progress slowed. Then disaster struck. Two of their guides decamped, taking some supplies with them, and bandits stole five of their animals. Then, suddenly, Charlie, who had been teething, died. They mournfully buried him but kept on.

They finally reached Nagqu, close to where Annie Taylor had been turned back, and they, too, were refused permission to continue. Rahmin, who had been travelling with them to return to his home, left them. Tibetan officials appointed an escort to take them to Ta-Chien-lu, but several days after starting they were ambushed by bandits. One of the Tibetans was shot in the arm, and some horses were stolen, others shot. Their guides, understandably, fled. Left with a heap of luggage, no animals to carry it, no guides to lead them and the likely return of the bandits, the Rijnharts abandoned most of their gear and trudged on. Shortly afterwards, they came within hailing distance of an encampment, on the other side of the fast-flowing Tsa Chu (Za Qu). They agreed that Petrus should try to cross the river to get assistance. He waded in, came back to shore and shouted out something Susie couldn't hear, then walked along the river's edge until he was out of sight. He never returned.

Susie, alone and frightened, waited for several days, then managed to get the Tibetans from the camp to help her cross the river. Inquiries at the camp were fruitless; no one, it seemed, had seen her husband. She hired two treacherous guides, using the promise of her telescope and a glimpse of her revolver to keep them in line until she reached a small lamasery, where a sympathetic Chinese merchant got her a passport, assuring her safe passage to the border.

Ta-Chien-lu in the 1880s.
The River of Golden Sand by Captain William Gill, London: John Murray, 1883, 169.

Two months after Petrus's disappearance, after sleeping rough, wearing her boots through, nearly starving and being threatened by drunken thieves, she arrived at Ta-Chien-lu and was delivered to the house of a missionary, Mr. Turner. Two men were standing in the courtyard as she walked in. "How clean they looked in Chinese garb," she recalled, "and how white their faces! I knew I was not clean, yet, conscious of my dirtiness and rags, I stood in their presence waiting to be addressed. But no, I must speak first; so I said in English, 'Is this Mr. Turner's?' and Mr. Moyes replied 'Yes.'"[16]

She had just met her next husband, Dr. James Moyes, though they didn't marry until 1905. She waited for six months, futilely hoping to hear word of Petrus's fate, then made her way back to Canada. She returned to Ta-Chien-lu in 1902 and continued her medical and missionary work. By 1908, because of her declining health, she and Moyes had returned to Canada, where she died.

Tibet continued to lure missionaries and explorers, all intent on reaching Lhasa. Although her journeys took place in the twentieth century and are therefore outside the scope of this book, it is worth mentioning that Alexandra David-Néel, author of *My Journey to Lhasa* (1927), was the first European woman to enter Lhasa. David-Néel, a Frenchwoman who became a reporter in India, was commissioned to interview the Dalai Lama. She entered Lhasa in 1923 and subsequently devoted her life to Tibetan causes.[17]

North America
Trollopizing a Continent

AS NEW AND UPSTART COLONIES, Canada and the United States were filled with lonely men who had money to burn. The anonymous male author of *Cariboo* (1862), about British Columbia's gold fields, urged young women to come out, not as teachers or governesses, but as wives. "I never saw diggers so desirous of marrying as those of British Columbia," he claimed.[1] At the time, there were two hundred men to every woman. This kind of publicity convinced many European women to make the long and tedious voyage to North America, on the chance they could hook one of these deserving fellows and turn them into decent husbands.

CANADA

Anna Jameson was different: she went to Canada in 1836 to lose her husband. He was Robert Jameson, the attorney general of Upper Canada (now Ontario). The couple had already been living apart, separated by the Atlantic Ocean; her ten-month stay resulted in a formal parting and also yielded her book *Winter Studies and Summer Rambles in Canada* (1838). In it, she described her inauspicious arrival at Toronto in December:

> What Toronto may be in summer, I cannot tell; they say it is a pretty place. At present its appearance to me, a stranger, is most strangely mean and melancholy. A little ill-built town on low land, at the bottom of a frozen bay, with one very ugly church . . . some government offices, built . . . in the most tasteless, vulgar style imaginable; three feet of snow all around . . . I did not expect much, but for this I was not prepared. Perhaps no preparation could have *prepared* me.[2]

Holed up in her Toronto house, she watched her ink freeze as she began translating a weighty German work on Goethe. She diverted herself with thoughts of past travels to Austria and Italy and, possibly, with

Fanny Trollope. Drawn by Miss L. Adams, engraved by W. Holl, *Domestic Manners of Americans* (1845 edition), frontispiece.

the potential in her misery for a story. She was appalled by her boredom: "To me it is something new, for I have never yet been *ennuyéed* to *death*—except in fiction."★ It was a miserable experience that not even Niagara Falls could appease; her disappointment in them was overwhelming.[3]

The snow eventually melted, and Jameson looked forward to exploring for two months. She travelled by carriage through the forests along roads that scarcely deserved to be called footpaths. Still, she kept her humour and excitement and made the most of the short summer. First she went back to Niagara Falls and made her peace with the place. She took several pages to express her inability to describe the sublime beauty of the falls and then headed to Detroit via Buffalo, Hamilton, Paris, Woodstock, London and Chatham.[4]

Her adventures came alive when she left Detroit on the steamer *Jefferson,* hoping to find a way to Sault Ste. Marie. The steamer dropped her off at Mackinaw (Mackinac) Island, where she discovered an acute shortage of accommodation. The certainty that things would work out washed over her: "With a sense of enjoyment keen and unanticipative as that of a child—looking

★Jameson wrote the novel-cum-travel book *The Diary of an Ennuyée* (1826).

neither before nor after—I soon abandoned myself to the present, and all its delicious exciting novelty, leaving the future to take care of itself." And it did; she was given a room at the house of a local agent.[5]

One of her goals was to meet native people, and this wish was amply satisfied on Mackinaw and, later, on Manitoulin. Much of the last third of her account describes the Chippewa and their legends. She's impressed with the status of women, discouraged by the predilection for drinking and, on one occasion, shocked by the natural state of ceremonial dancers:

> When these wild and more than half-naked figures came up, leaping, whooping, drumming, shrieking, hideously painted, and flourishing clubs, tomahawks, javelins, it was like a masque of fiends breaking into paradise! . . . Of their style of clothing, I say nothing—for, as it is wisely said, nothing can come of *nothing:*—only if 'all symbols be clothes,' according to our great modern philosopher . . . my Indian friends were as little symbolical as you can dare to imagine:—*passons par là.*[6]

She left Mackinaw a week later in a canoe paddled by five voyageurs. During the two-day trip to Sault Ste. Marie, her awe was marred only by the swarms of mosquitoes. The first week in August she returned to Toronto, again by canoe, in the company of twenty-one men, whom she called her "cavaliers." They respected her privacy and one morning laid out her breakfast, complete with a bouquet of flowers.[7] She could not think of a better destination than Canada for those world-wearied travellers who had exhausted Europe:

Anna Jameson, somewhat older than when she travelled through Canada's wilderness in 1837. Duyckinck, vol. 2, facing p. 12.

> I wonder how it is that some of those gentry whom I used to see in London, looking as though they would give an empire for new pleasure or a new sensation, do not come here. If epicures, they should come to eat white-fish and beavers' tails; if sportsmen, here is a very paradise for bear-hunting, deer-hunting, otter-hunting;—and wild-fowl in thousands, and fish in shoals; and if they be contemplative lovers of the picturesque, *blasés* with Italy and

Shooting the Rapids, c. 1879, near Lachine, Quebec, by Frances Anne Hopkins. Oil on canvas. Frances Anne and her husband are seated in the centre of the canoe.
Courtesy National Archives of Canada (1989-401-2X; C-2774).

elbowed out of Switzerland, let them come here and find the true philosopher's stone—or rather the true elixir of life—*novelty!*[8]

Jameson returned to England, where she became a respected art historian. Her other travel books included *Sketches in Canada and Rambles Among the Red Men* (1852) and *Camping in Colorado with Suggestions to Gold-Seekers, Tourists and Invalids* (1879).

Frances Anne Hopkins shared Jameson's delight in the Canadian wilderness. An artist, she came to Canada from England with her husband—the private secretary to the governor of the Hudson's Bay Company—and travelled with him, largely by canoe, for some ten years. She sketched and painted majestic landscapes as well as the daily scenes of camp life. She returned to England in 1870.

A number of women emigrated to Canada; sisters Susanna Moodie and Catherine Parr Traill were two celebrated pioneers. Two other, less well known ones were Scots: Isabel Gunn and Letitia Hargrave; both came to Canada through the offices of the Hudson's Bay Company.

For many years, the Hudson's Bay Company only hired men, a

condition neatly sidestepped by Gunn, who called herself John Fubbister, possibly as a means of seeking adventure or perhaps in hot pursuit of a deceitful lover. She was sent to Fort Albany in the summer of 1806, performed her work there credibly for a year, then was sent to Pembina, on the Red River. She was presumably not able to track down the errant lover, if he indeed existed. She found a substitute, however, and in the winter of 1807, to everyone's surprise, John Fubbister had a baby. John became Mary, donned women's clothes and returned to Fort Albany, where she continued to work until the company, in compliance with its "no white women" policy, could send her home. She left, against her will, in the fall of 1809.[9]

The Hudson's Bay Company ships Prince Albert *(left) and* Prince Rupert *(right). The ships, which carried passengers, mail, supplies and furs, were lifelines for the residents at the factories. ILN, 21 June 1845: 388.*

Letitia Mactavish Hargrave had been fetched, so to speak, by a lonely employee at York Factory, a fur-trading town on the shores of remote Hudson Bay. James Hargrave courted her by the mails, then came and got her in 1840. Barely prepared for the trip from her home in Argyllshire, Scotland, to London, let alone a voyage across the Atlantic, she suffered travel fatigue, sore throat, headaches and stomach disorders. Her cheery letters thinly disguised her woe.

Her first reaction on arrival, after an uncomfortable passage on the *Prince Rupert,* was to cry herself "sick." Amazingly, she took well to her new home, and her letters became bright and informative, describing the various hierarchies in the company and local society, the fluid marriages between white men and native women (and the resulting offspring) and, of course, everyone's health, or lack thereof. Her letters, not intended for publication, are lively and surprisingly frank. In one letter to her husband, who was away temporarily, she wrote that a guest, Miss Sinclair, spoke in her sleep of having been raped: "She wound up very philosophically with the remark that that was a common thing, her sister & Miss MacKenzie having experienced a similar misfortune. I don't like to tell her that she talks in her sleep especially that she is so peculiar in her choice of subjects."[10]

The Hargraves had five children, one of whom died shortly after birth; the others flourished. She and her family made two visits home, in 1846 and 1851, to arrange for schooling for two of her children. When she returned from this second trip it was to make a new home in Sault Ste. Marie. She died from cholera two years later at the age of forty-one.

It is unlikely that Ida Pfeiffer would have ever become well disposed towards Canada, given her rude reception at Montreal and Quebec City in 1854. She attributed the foul attitude, especially by innkeepers, to her lowly status as lone female. After being turned away from one Montreal hotel, she managed to get a room at another by showing the colour of her money. On the street, her requests for directions were greeted with sullen "don't knows." "Certainly," she wrote, "it did not appear to me that courtesy to strangers could be numbered among the Canadian virtues."[11] She couldn't get away fast enough.

Isabella Bird, who was in Canada the same year as Pfeiffer, left with a more favourable opinion, having more thoroughly explored the country. She arrived in Halifax and toured Nova Scotia, Prince Edward Island, New Brunswick, Ontario and Quebec. Her way was smoothed slightly through connections, and she was only twenty-three, much younger than Pfeiffer. This was also her first big adventure, and she arrived game to tackle every unsprung carriage, bumpy corduroy road and appalling meal the young country could throw at her.

THE UNITED STATES

The United States, having been civilized for a much longer time, attracted far more travellers than Canada. Frances (Fanny) Trollope, author of *Domestic Manners of the Americans* (1832), a scathing denouncement of American customs, set the tone for travel writers for decades to come. The book was published at the end of her four-year sojourn, from 1827 to 1831, during which time Trollope travelled widely and tried her hand at various ambitious but unsuccessful entrepreneurial efforts, including novelty museums and an extravagant shopping bazaar in Cincinnati that came to be known locally as Trollope's Folly.[12]

Trollope attacked slavery and mercilessly derided what she saw as American boorishness. Entertaining details such as her description of Cincinnati's garbage collectors—pigs that ate the trash thrown into the middle of the street—filled the pages. (Over twenty years later, Isabella Bird, another witness to this system, pointed out that the city was also known as Porkopolis.) Trollope tried to be fair, taking time to admire features such as New York's harbour, but of Americans she could only conclude that "of the population generally, as seen in town and country, among the rich and the poor, in the slave states, and the free states . . . I do not like them. I do not like their principles, I do not like their manners, I do not like their opinions."[13]

A view of Cincinnati. Seen from a distance, the city doesn't look nearly as bad as Fanny Trollope described. ILN, 7 June 1845: 356.

Trollope returned to England in 1831, hoping to make enough money through writing to pay back the debts from her failed American ventures. When *Domestic Manners* went to four editions in the first year and received great publicity from attacks in caricature, print and side shows, it looked as though she'd suceeded. But in spite of this success, she and her husband, Tom, who had been keeping the home fires burning while she was abroad, had to flee to the Continent in 1834 to escape creditors. There she wrote many more travel books, including *Belgium and Western Germany in 1833, Paris and the Parisians in 1835, Vienna and the Austrians* and *A Visit to Italy*. She was also, like her son Anthony, a successful and prolific novelist. She eventually overcame her financial battles and continued to travel. She died in comfortable surroundings in Florence in October 1863, eighty-three years old.

On the verge of bankruptcy before her American adventure, Trollope had been talked into going to the United States by Fanny Wright, a fiery Scottish social reformer and abolitionist. Wright was also an aspiring playwright and a wealthy heiress who, as a girl, had come to view the United States as a promised land. With her sister, Camilla, she arrived in New York on the *Amity* in August 1818 and stayed until 1820. *Views and Society and Manners in America . . . by an Englishwoman* (1821) was the result of her travels, the enthusiastic observations of a breathless Americaphile tempered by criticisms of slavery and women's fashions and habits. Unlike Trollope's book, hers was well received in the United States.

Wright returned in 1824; this time she and her sister accompanied the French rebel leader of the War of Independence, the Marquis de Lafayette, to whom she'd been introduced by Trollope. A noted womanizer, Lafayette, now sixty-seven, could still be considered a risky companion, and Wright's relationship with him provoked nasty gossip.

Wright's social consciousness drove her to buy some land near Memphis, Tennessee, which she called Nashoba, and a number of slaves, with the idea of preparing them for freedom. She herself laboured there until malaria and sunstroke forced her to stop. After a brief visit to France in 1827, she returned to Nashoba with Trollope and found her estate in chaos and Camilla married. Trollope, appalled at the squalor, fled as soon as she could. Wright later freed her slaves and took them to Haiti. She then turned to lecturing on the benefits of sexual equality and birth control, provoking Trollope to call her the "advocate of opinions that make millions shudder."[14]

In 1831, several months after the death of her sister, Wright married Phiquepal d'Arusmont, a French educational theorist, who had been her travelling companion for several years and with whom she had a daughter. Not much is known of her life after this point, except that she was continuously reviled for her idealistic and progressive views, that she virtually commuted between the United States and Europe and that d'Arusmont was a rascal who cheated money from both wife and daughter.[15]

Another abolitionist, Harriet Martineau, came to the United States in August 1834. Martineau, whom we last saw in Egypt advising ladies to iron away their Nile cruise, had a relatively uneventful forty-two–day Atlantic crossing, save for the loss of a sheep, which jumped overboard, thereby depriving the passengers of mutton. As they approached New York, the harbour pilot came alongside and inquired of the captain if a well-known abolitionist was on board. He was not, so the pilot then discreetly asked about Martineau, and if it was thought that she'd raise a fuss, as there had recently been serious anti-abolitionist riots in New York. A passenger assured him that though Martineau was against slavery "in principle," she was going to the United States "to learn and not to teach." Martineau was later shown a newspaper article announcing her arrival and exhorting "readers not to chew tobacco or praise themselves" if she was around.[16] They were still smarting from Trollope's slap in the face.

Martineau's goal in travelling to North America, as a journalist and social reformer, was to report on the living conditions in the United States. Because her writings and opinions were already known, she was greeted with suspicion. But she also received enviable invitations, her luggage was exempted from customs examination and the outpouring of hospitality was remarkable. Clearly, she and her unidentified lady companion were to be treated with kid gloves, and judging from the name dropping that followed, she repaid the favours many times over.

Martineau tiptoed through the United States. For every nasty thing she wrote about Americans (their men spat nauseatingly and their women rocked their chairs dizzyingly), she found something to praise or countered with insults about the English. (English visitors especially were trashed.) And in the face of America's prosperity, she was ashamed at Britain's failure to pull Canada out of its wild and uncultured state. "How absurd it was that poor country should belong to us," she wrote, "its poverty and hopeless inactivity contrasting, so much to our disgrace, with the prosperous activity of the opposite shore."[18]

Like Trollope, she experienced a full American winter, and she visited Baltimore, Philadelphia and Washington, D.C. Then, though she had been warned that Southerners were incensed by her views, she headed to New Orleans, through the Carolinas, Georgia and Alabama. From New Orleans she travelled north to Cincinnati, which she proclaimed the American city that she would most like to live in. This point appears to be a direct salvo at Trollope, who upon leaving that city in 1830 wrote, "I believe there was not one of our party who did not experience a sensation of pleasure in leaving it." Their only regret, she added, was that they had ever gone there in the first place.[19]

Martineau travelled in stagecoaches, admitting that they caused fatigue but that she enjoyed them all the same. Rest stops were frustratingly brief, but she learned to make the most of them, sometimes choosing to sleep rather than eat. The speed required to prepare for a nap at a coach inn meant that the ladies would rush in with their night caps, soap and towels already in hand, anxiously looking for someone to show them their room and fetch some water. As the minutes ticked away, the slowness of the servants, who felt no need to hurry, became agonizing. Once the ladies had undressed and washed up, they fell onto the beds, quickly dealing with dirty sheets and drafts of cold air by wrapping themselves up in their dressing gowns and cloaks. Then "as soon as they are fairly dreaming that they are at home, and need not get up till they please, the horn startles them, they raise their heads, see a light under the door, and the black woman looks in to drawl out that they must please to make haste. It seems like a week since they lay down; but they are not rested."[20]

When Martineau met a bookseller who declared himself ready to publish whatever she wrote about

> "Among the strongest of the fresh feelings excited by foreign travel,—those fresh feelings which are an actual reinforcement of life,—is that of welcome surprise at the sympathy the traveller is able to yield, as well as privileged to receive."
> —Harriet Martineau[17]

America, she protested that she had no plans for a book. He assured her that she must have plenty of material and suggested that she "Trollopize a bit" to make it readable. In the end, she managed to produce two hefty works, *Retrospect of Western Travel* (1838) and *Society in America* (1839). Both received rave reviews in Britain but far less enthusiasm in the United States. *Society in America* covered politics, slavery and social issues; *Retrospect* dealt mainly with travel, though there were chapters on prisons, slavery and the mute and blind. It ended oddly, with a chapter on cemeteries. "The dead, it is hoped," Martineau wrote, "are entering on a new region, in which they are to act with fresh powers and a wiser activity. The refreshed traveller has the same ambition."[21] A unique, one hopes, view of travel.

Emmeline Wortley and her twelve-year-old daughter, Victoria, were less critical visitors to the United States. Apparently delighted with all she saw, Emmeline was nevertheless an attentive and pithy observer, as can be seen in her book *Travels in the United States, etc.* (1851). Victoria, too, published an account. *Young Traveller's Journal of a Tour in North and South America* (1852) probably made her the youngest travel writer ever, male or female.

Emmeline, Victoria and two maids arrived in New York on the *Canada* in May 1849 and set out to explore the East Coast from Niagara to New Orleans, followed by Mexico and Peru. In her preface, Emmeline announced her intentions to write for those who enjoy "the gossip of travel," and the book is filled with descriptions of dinners, conversations and chance encounters. To mark the occasion of visits to such places as the Mammoth Cave in Kentucky, she wrote poetry, having already established herself as a poet through frequent contributions to *Blackwood's*. She met the crème de la crème of society, as well as naturalist Louis Agassiz, during her stay in Cambridge, Massachusetts. Agassiz, along with Washington Irving, Longfellow and the Mormons, became the American tourist attraction equivalent of Byron and Staël. Wortley was also introduced to several women travellers and admired their endurance: "American ladies, perhaps, on the whole do not travel about as much as we do, but when they do set about it, the uttermost ends of the earth seem scarcely to alarm them."[22]

"Washington would be a beautiful city if it were built; but as it is not I can not say much about it."
—Emmeline Wortley[23]

Niagara Falls in Winter.

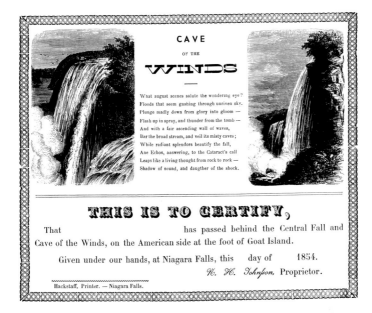

CAVE

OF THE

WINDS

—

What august scenes salute the wondering eye?
Floods that seem gushing through unriven sky.
Plunge madly down from glory into gloom —
Flash up in spray, and thunder from the tomb —
And with a fair ascending wall of waves,
Bar the broad stream, and veil its misty caves;
While radiant splendors beautify the fall,
Ane Echos, answering, to the Cataract's call
Leaps like a living thought from rock to rock —
Shadow of sound, and daugther of the shock.

THIS IS TO CERTIFY,

That   has passed behind the Central Fall and
Cave of the Winds, on the American side at the foot of Goat Island.

Given under our hands, at Niagara Falls, this   day of   1854.

H. H. Johnson, Proprietor.

Hackstaff, Printer. — Niagara Falls.

Wortley and all of the other travellers discussed here made the obligatory visit—or visits, in Martineau's and Jameson's case—to Niagara Falls. Martineau, like the others, went into raptures at the sight but cautioned that "to offer an idea of Niagara by writing of hues and dimensions is much like representing the kingdom of Heaven by images of jasper and topazes." Her friend Sara Coleridge enjoyed her description in *Retrospect,* declaring that it "gives one a most lively *waterfallish* feeling."[24]

Trollope was less poetic and more energetic in her description of the falls: "We passed four delightful days of excitement and fatigue; we drenched ourselves in spray; we cut our feet on the rocks; we blistered our faces in the sun; we looked up the cataract, and down the cataract; we perched ourselves on every pinnacle we could find; we dipped our fingers in the flood at a few yards' distance from its thundering fall; in short, we strove to fill as many inches of memory with Niagara, as possible; and I think the images will be within the power of recall for ever."[25] Naturally, she preferred the falls on the Canadian side.

Bird hazarded a foray behind the falls at the insistence of friends who themselves refused to go. She completely changed from her dress and shoes into an oiled calico frock and rubbers, then was led through mud to rickety stairs, which she descended in great trepidation. At the bottom, she and

A certificate acknowledging that the bearer had braved Niagara Falls' "Cave of the Winds." Isabella Bird earned such a document when she succeeded in going behind the falls. Tour du monde 3, 1861: 260.

Niagara Falls in winter. Postcard, pre-1904.

Isabella Bird, from A Lady's Life in the Rocky Mountains, *1910, title page. Bird had this sketch added to later editions of her book (first published in 1879) to counteract comments by the press that she had worn men's attire.*

her guide proceeded along a narrow path, buffeted by gusts of wind. Fear overtook her, and she shouted that she wanted to go back. The roar of the water drowned out her words, but her guide, who was black, offered his hand to steady her. Bird, with an aversion common at the time, hesitated momentarily, but once she took his hand, she held on as tightly as she could. When her pleas to return finally became audible, her guide just shook his head and yelled that going back was worse. When she reached the end, she reflected that there was "nothing whatever to boast of in having accomplished it."[26]

The spitting habit elicited almost as much comment as Niagara. Pfeiffer, who felt she could take just about anything, was disgusted to see well-dressed Californian gents expectorating in public. But it was not nearly as bad as their other practice, "still more abominable . . . though they carried a pocket-handkerchief, of making use of their fingers instead of it." On account of the spitting, Trollope decided the word "gentlemen" was overused and inaccurate. Bird was aghast at the number of spittoons that furnished salons in hotels and boats, and how ineffective they were at keeping the floors free of noxious puddles of tobacco juice.[27]

Bird's second and most memorable trip to North America took her to Colorado in 1873–74 and resulted in *A Lady's Life in the Rocky Mountains* (1879). She arrived in San Francisco from the Sandwich Islands and headed for the Rocky Mountains as soon as possible. A greater contrast couldn't have been imagined. She had come from a lush, warm paradise with a comfortable mix of men and women to cold, remote mountains where there were few women about, and those who were there could tell a racy story every bit as well as a man.

After several thwarted attempts, Bird finally rode a pack horse into unsurveyed and untrampled Estes Park (north of Boulder), hunkered down for the bitterly cold winter as housekeeper for a couple of poorly provisioned hunters and even commenced a doomed romance with a self-admitted ruffian, trapper "Mountain Jim" Nugent. Although she was tempted to stay on, the cold and privations became too trying, so in December she left as she had originally planned. She met with rough but kind hospitality everywhere she went; at Boulder she asked to hire a horse and overheard the owner reply, "If it's the English lady travelling in the mountains, she can have a horse, but not any one else."[28]

"Twenty Minutes for Lunch." Isabella Bird wrote about the crush of the finding and eating of meals, during the brief stops at North American railway stations.[29] This inconvenience ended once onboard meal service was instituted.
Graphic, 14 April 1877: 332.

Marianne North, who had visited the east in 1871, toured the western United States in 1875. This trip resembled many of her others—vast distances covered in a flurry of visits and impressions. She hastened from Chicago to Salt Lake City, where she paused long enough to reluctantly shake Brigham Young's hand. Then she visited Yosemite, San Francisco, Lake Tahoe and Virginia City and was on board the *Oceanic* bound for Japan some six weeks later. She returned in 1881, for a similarly breakneck tour.

We briefly met Lola Montez, the fiery Spanish dancer, in India, in the person of pretty Eliza James, wife of Lieutenant James, and the darling of Simla's 1839 season. Between then and her arrival in New York on the *Humboldt* in November 1851, she managed to effect a startling transformation.

Eliza, it turned out, didn't much like living with James; she left him and returned to Britain, clutching £1000 of her stepfather's money. She had the idea of taking up a genteel occupation, but before her ship had docked, she had hooked up with a George Lennox. Soon the pair were openly living together, freely spending her allowance. James heard of her scandalous behaviour and successfully sued for divorce.

She took off to Cádiz and rematerialized as the daughter of an exiled Spanish nobleman and widow of a recently executed rebel, styling herself Maria Dolores de Porris y Montez, or Lola for short. Her début back in England was as a fiery, black-haired, blue-eyed dancer, the likes of which had never been seen on the British stage. The press gave her ample coverage, and benefactors gravitated to her, as did audiences, in spite of her amateur attempts at dancing. But never far from scandal, Lola was denounced as a fraudulent Eliza, and in the summer of 1843 she left for the Continent.[30]

The Humboldt, *in which Lola Montez sailed, was wrecked in 1853, at the entrance to the Halifax harbour. It was described as a "fine first-class steamer," in the* Illustrated London News' *article about the ship's demise. J.F. Bland,* ILN, *31 December 1853: 593.*

At this point Montez's travels really began. From then until the end of her life she barely kept still; she travelled across Germany, Poland, Russia, Germany again, France, Belgium, Italy, Switzerland, Spain, the United States, Australia, back to the United States, Europe and finally America again. Her life reads like a catalogue of the best hotels and steamships, and on her travels she took up with such luminaries as composer Franz Liszt, diplomat Robert Peel and, most important, Ludwig I, King of Bavaria.[31]

It's not clear how Montez maintained her lifestyle. But

after she arrived in Munich in October 1846 and captivated the king, her finances were amply taken care of, at least for a while. Ludwig paid her a stipend, which she overspent in lavish entertaining and furnishing of her home. Unchecked, she could have easily drained Bavaria dry. Because of the king's blind passion for her (in spite of evidence of her infidelity), she was not only made a citizen of Bavaria but also named a countess, and thus tore the kingdom asunder, forced ministers to resign and, for a time, turned citizens against their beloved king.

In the face of riots, Ludwig regretfully begged her to leave, and in February 1848, she departed for Switzerland. Montez and the king continued to correspond, and she risked a surreptitious return to Munich disguised as a young man, complete with a beard. When word got out that she was back, the citizens went wild. Ludwig was forced to exile her, and he abdicated in favour of his son Maximilian II.[32]

If this first half of Montez's life has been difficult to summarize, the second half is even harder. Her romantic attachments became more entangled as she juggled Ludwig and other admirers with a bigamous marriage. (Her divorce did not allow her to remarry.) She took to the stage again, in 1851, and her performances in New York that year drew huge audiences. At one performance more than three thousand people showed up, though of that number only about thirty were women. Even in the New World, Montez was considered too risqué. She settled for a time in California, then assembled a troupe and went to Australia in 1855. When she returned to America a year later she had assumed a religious tone and gave a series of sold-out lectures on beauty, fashion and gallantry. In 1859, she toured Britain, lecturing on the United States, criticizing abolitionists and attacking the women's movement. Back in the United States in late 1859, she continued her speaking tours but fell ill in the summer of 1860, possibly of a stroke. She hung on until 17 January 1861.

But in 1853, long before her death, Lola Montez, along with hundreds of other women, had made the difficult journey across the Isthmus of Panama, at that time the easiest way to travel from the East Coast to California. For some, this route was a once-in-a-lifetime chance for a Central American experience.

Central & South America *Not for Namby-Pambies*

CENTRAL AMERICA

The day Lola Montez swaggered into the Panamanian town of Gorgona, hotel owner Mary Seacole, saw a fine-looking, "bad-eyed" woman sporting a gent's suit, with "a velvet lapelled coat, richly worked shirt-front, black hat, French unmentionables, and natty, polished boots with spurs." Montez also carried a whip, which she used on a bold American who had grabbed hold of her coat tails. The slash he received on his face, observed Seacole, "must have marked him for some days." She wasn't the only one glad to see Montez leave the next morning. The owner of the overcrowded hotel where Montez put up that night—not Seacole—was intimidated into rustling up a cot for her dog, Flora. When he tried to bill her $5 for the extra bed, she brandished her pistol to get the charge lowered.[1]

Montez's stormy passage across the Isthmus of Panama in the spring of 1853 fuelled her reputation as a firebrand. If one can believe Seacole, the women who made the crossing were a motley crew. They dressed in men's clothing and could only be distinguished from the men by their "bolder and more reckless voice and manner."[2]

Before she set up in the Crimea, where we met her last, Mary Seacole had established two hotels on the route across Panama, cashing in on the gold-rush fever that sent hordes rushing to California. She joined her brother, who ran the Independent Hotel at Cruces in 1850, and there found enough business to open up a hotel across the street. Her hotel rarely took overnight lodgers but rather specialized in refreshments. When cholera broke out, Seacole nursed many victims back to health or provided sympathy to those who weren't going to make it. She may be the first woman ever to have conducted a post-mortem on a cholera victim in the jungles of Panama. She came down with the disease herself but pulled through, then moved to nearby

Lola Montez. From a painting by Joseph Stieler, 1847, commissioned by Ludwig I of Bavaria. *Lola Montez* by Edmund d'Auvergne, New York: Brentano, 1909, frontispiece.

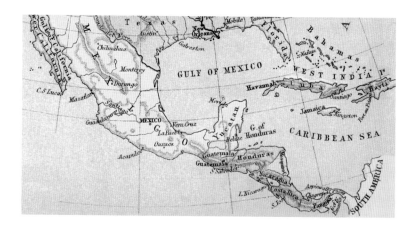

Gorgona and built a ladies-only hotel—which could be why Montez, clearly no lady, didn't stay with her.

Seacole may also have run into Emmeline and Victoria Wortley as they passed through Cruces in 1850. Before the Wortleys arrived in Panama, they had caught a steamer from New Orleans to Vera Cruz and had travelled across Mexico by diligence to Mexico City and back again. They caught another steamer to Havana and from there sailed to Chagres on the east coast of Panama. This was the toughest and most interesting part of their trip, as they made their way to the west coast by canoe and mule. Wortley compared the canoe to the cage that must have held Mrs. Noble during her imprisonment in China.[3] From Panama, the Wortleys sailed south by steamer to Peru. Then, not satisfied with having made the gruesome crossing once, they retraced their path from Peru to Chagres and caught another steamer to Jamaica, where her account ended.

Mexico is not well documented by women travellers, making Wortley's account important. Of even more value, because of the length of time she spent in Mexico, were the observations of Frances Erskine Inglis, or, as she was known after her marriage, Mme Calderón de la Barca. Joined by her French maid and her maid's French poodle, Calderón accompanied her husband, Don Angel Calderón de la Barca, in his role as Spanish envoy to Mexico City in October 1839. They sailed to Vera Cruz, then travelled overland to Mexico City. Her dry and witty descriptions of travel took the form of letters to family and were published as

Life in Mexico, During a Residence of Two Years in that Country (1843). The *Quarterly Review* accused her of keeping the reader at arm's length, while they acknowledged her to be spirited and intelligent.[4]

The Calderóns' status ensured a high level of comfort and luxury for their travels, but in Mexico luxury was a relative term. Calderón weighed their options—coach, *litera* or diligence—for getting overland from Vera Cruz to the capital:

Diligence travel in Mexico. *ILN*, 1 February 1845: 68.

"The diligence goes in four days, if it does not break down. The coach takes any time we choose over that; the *literas* nine or ten days, going slowly on mules with a sedan-chair motion. The diligence has food and beds provided for it at the inns—the others nothing. I am in favour of the diligence."[5]

They made it to Mexico City without incident, only to be greeted with the threat of revolution, which indeed came to pass during their stay. Uprisings notwithstanding, they made frequent forays to other towns, which were close by our standards but at the time required several days of tiring travel.

Calderón looked Mexico in the eye, refusing to gloss over the regular reports of murders and robberies. She watched the branding of seven hundred bellowing bulls unflinchingly and then wrote: "Such roaring, such shouting, such an odour of singed hair and *biftek au naturel,* such playing of music, and such wanton risks as were run by the men!" And of bullfights, to which other, more delicate women closed their eyes in disgust, she exclaimed, "Another bull-fight last evening! . . . One makes wry faces at it at first, and then begins to like it."[6]

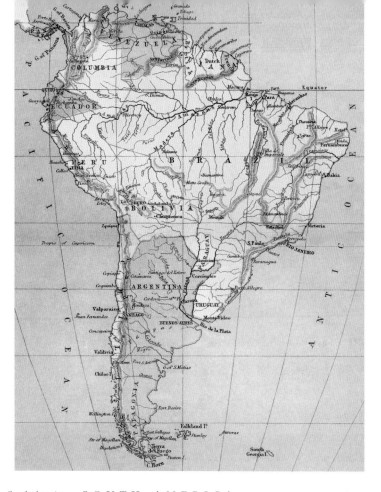

SOUTH AMERICA

Two travellers to South America, specifically to Surinam on the north coast, are interesting, not only because of the early dates at which they travelled, but because of their remarkable lives as well. The first, English playwright Aphra Behn, probably best known for her role as a spy, told her account in the form of the autobiographical novel *Orinooko*. The other, German botanical artist and entomologist Maria Sibylla Merian, left only sketchy details for historians to piece together.

Behn was described in a brief biography from 1735 as a "Gentlewoman by Birth," whose father, given a post—perhaps that of lieutenant-governor—in Surinam, took his wife and children, including Behn, with him. He died on the voyage over; Behn and her family stayed for a short time in Surinam before returning to England. The biographer claimed that untrue aspersions were cast on Behn's moral character and that she quickly returned to England for no other reason than to report to Charles II on his

South American territory. At his urging, apparently, she wrote *Orinooko: Or, The Royal Slave,* as an account of her experiences. Told in the first person, the novel tells of an African prince who is sold into slavery and brought to Surinam to work on the plantations. Some details of Behn's personal life slip in, such as a mention of her house on St. John's Hill.[7]

A recent Behn biographer, Maureen Duffy, examined the possibility that Behn never went to Surinam; the details in *Orinooko* could have been cribbed from accounts of the time. On the basis of private correspondence, however, Duffy was convinced that Behn did go. And if she did, she would have been there from August 1663 until February 1664. England and France had been trying to establish colonies in the region since the 1640s, and in spite of the natives people's efforts to pry the foreigners off their land, by the 1660s there was a fairly sizable European community; the Dutch took it over in 1667, and it became Dutch Guiana.[8]

Aphra Behn.
Behn, *The Plays, Histories, and Novels,*
1871, vol. 1, frontispiece.

Nearly forty years later, Merian went to Dutch Guiana to study, collect and paint tropical insects. With her twenty-one-year-old daughter Dorothea, also a painter, she set sail in June 1699 and arrived late summer. They settled in Paramaribo, and with the help of slaves and a native couple, she collected a phenomenal number of insects. Biographer Natalie Zemon Davis points out that her achievement was unusual, not only because she was a female, but because naturalists normally accompanied expeditions.[9]

But Merian was an unusual person. She was born in Frankfurt to a family of artist/publishers, married an engraver and, between 1675 and 1680, published several important botanical works. She separated from her husband in 1685 and joined a religious movement in Friesland. A few years later, she resumed her maiden name, moved to Amsterdam and picked up where she had left off, painting, teaching and collecting. The decision to go to South America seemed to have been driven by a desire to learn of New

World tropical insects. Financed through the sales of her paintings and specimens, she was able to remain in Dutch Guiana for two years. When the climate began to take its toll on her health, she packed it in and returned to Amsterdam, where she wrote, produced, published and marketed the results of her studies, *Metamorphosis of the Insects* (1705).[10]

Seventy years after Merian's visit to Dutch Guiana, Isabella Godin des Odonais was fighting her way along the Amazon, trying to reach her husband, Jean, who was a member of Charles-Marie de la Condamine's expedition to determine the shape of the earth. The Godins had been stationed at Quito in 1748, when Jean received word of the death of his father in Paris. He was obliged to return, and Isabella, who was Peruvian and had long wished to see her husband's homeland, decided to go too.* But she was pregnant—she often was—and the voyage through the jungle was considered too risky, so Jean took off in March 1749, with the expectation that she would follow later. At Cayenne he ordered transport for her to be ready at such time as she could leave. Unfortunately, the men to whom he entrusted the arrangements were incompetent, and Isabella was forced to organize her departure herself. The process was clearly time consuming, as she didn't leave until October 1769.[11]

She travelled with her two brothers, a nephew, three Frenchmen, servants and thirty-one porters. They arranged for provisions to await them at the thriving town of Canelos, but when they reached it a month later it had been ravaged by smallpox. Their porters abandoned them. They built a canoe with the help of two surviving villagers, who also consented to pilot the boat, but two days later these pilots ran away. They found another pilot, then, only three days later, he fell into the river and drowned. They were helpless without anyone to steer the canoe, so two of the men, along with some servants, struck out through the jungle to find assistance. Godin and the others waited for a month, then built a raft and set off, but it hit a tree and sank. They continued on foot, lost and disoriented. Without food and overcome by

Isabella Godin, now dreadfully alone, is about to fight her way through the jungle. Dronsart, 11.

---

* Thus confirming Flora Tristan's observation referred to in the introduction that Peruvian women would go to any length to travel.

⤳Were it told in a romance that a female of delicate habit, accustomed to all the comforts of life, had been precipitated into a river; that, after being withdrawn when on the point of drowning, this female . . . had penetrated into the unknown and pathless woods, and travelled in them for weeks, not knowing whither she directed her steps; that, enduring hunger, thirst, and fatigue to very exhaustion she should have seen her two brothers, far more robust than her, a nephew yet a youth, three young women her servants, and a young man, the domestic left by the physician who had gone on before, all expire by her side, and she yet survive . . . the author would be charged with inconsistency; but the historian should paint facts to his readers, and this is nothing but the truth.[12]

fever, everyone except Godin died. Surrounded by the dead, choked with thirst and in rags, she picked herself up and fought through heavy undergrowth for the next eight days until she stumbled across some Amazonian Indians, who took her to the next town of Andoas. The trip was far from over, but now she was in more or less competent hands. She and her husband were reunited at the mouth of the Amazon.[13]

Four nineteenth-century travellers to South America were Maria Dundas Graham, Flora Tristan, Ida Pfeiffer and Isabel Burton. Graham documented her two sojourns in her books, *Journal of a Voyage to Brazil* and *Journal of a Residence in Chile* (1824). The Chilean book covers the untimely death of her beloved husband, Thomas, and her resolute efforts to stand on her own. Devoid of sentimentality, her account has a vigour that has withstood time.

The Grahams sailed from Plymouth to Rio de Janeiro in July 1821. Thomas, commander of the *Doris,* was to observe and protect British trade in South America during the Brazilian and Chilean struggles for independence. The posting gave Maria an unparalleled opportunity to view the political and the social conditions along the coast of Brazil, especially in Rio de Janeiro and Bahía Blanca. She reported on the effects of the Brazilian revolution on daily life, helped nurse members of their crew suffering from fevers and dysentery and ducked occasional skirmishes between factions.

Although Maria was tubercular, it was Thomas who fell ill in November 1822, as did many of the ship's crew. By mid-March, in spite of his continuing ill health, they were underway for Valparaiso. She hoped that the lower temperatures of Cape Horn would alleviate the general poor state of health on board, but the freezing conditions only made things worse. Thomas died on 8 April 1822 as they rounded the Cape; the *Doris* reached Valparaiso on the 28th.[14]

Maria had the choice of departing on an American ship or staying in Valparaiso; she decided to rent a small cottage on the outskirts of the city where she could try to overcome her grief and regain her health. Her sojourn was by no means a solitary one; aside from the Chilean and expatriate European friends she made and the comings and goings of the officers of the *Doris,* whom she considered family, her cousin Glennie, who also suffered from consumption, stayed with her occasionally. As well, she reestablished a friendship with Lord Cochrane, a former British officer, now admiral of the Chilean navy.[15]

Graham's routine of visiting, walking, sketching and writing in her journal was interrupted in July 1822 by a mild earthquake and in mid-August, by a series of excursions into the countryside and to Santiago and its environs. She returned to Valparaiso to nurse her ailing cousin, though she herself had been suffering from a recurrence of her tuberculosis. In November, a huge earthquake struck, and for Graham's remaining stay in Chile, the aftershocks and the devastation to the country made life extremely difficult. Valparaiso was very badly damaged, and her cottage, one of the few habitable dwellings left, was snatched out from under her by an English family. She left Chile in January 1823, for Bahía Blanca.

Her health deteriorated rapidly in Brazil, so she returned to England in October. Her journals were published the following year, and she went back to Rio to teach the empress's daughter, staying until 1826. Back in England, she worked as an editor for John Murray, then married landscape painter Augustus Callcott, whom she dragged all over Europe. She wrote nine more books, including her successful *Little Arthur's History of England* (1835). Her tuberculosis finally overcame her in 1842, and she died at the age of fifty-seven.

Flora Tristan, best known as a feminist, a reformer and Gaugin's grandmother, travelled to her father's homeland of Peru, in 1833–34, in an attempt to claim her inheritance. The outcome, *Mémoires et pérégrinations d'une paria (Peregrinations of a Pariah)* (1838), was an attack on her father's family intertwined with travelogue and social commentary.

Before her departure in February 1833, Tristan had left her violent husband, with whom she had had three children. Technically illegitimate, and thus not an eligible heiress, she still hoped to become self-sufficient by convincing her Peruvian uncle, Don Pio de Tristan, that she was owed her father's share of the estate. She boarded the *Mexicain* at Bordeaux and, during the 133-day voyage to Valparaiso, inadvertently captured the heart of the captain, Zacharie Chabrié. She was respected and cosseted by

the officers on the ship, but the rough seas, especially as they rounded Cape Horn, and Chabrié's constant attentions drained her of stamina.

From Valparaiso, where everyone turned out to see the "pretty young lady," she sailed to Islay on the coast of Peru, where she was plagued by fleas at a guest-house.[16] The next night the innkeeper, Mme Justo, showed her the ropes:

> She placed four or five chairs in a row with the last one next to the bed, and made me undress on the first. I proceeded to the second wearing only my shift, while Madame Justo took all my clothes out of the room, advising me to wipe myself with a towel to remove the fleas still clinging to my body. Then I went from chair to chair as far as the bed, where I put on a white nightgown liberally sprinkled with eau de cologne. This procedure gave me two hours of peace, but after that I could feel the fleas returning to the attack, thousands of them converging upon my bed.[17]

Tristan travelled by mule from Islay to Arequipa, where her uncle lived. The trek through desert and mountains nearly killed her. "I had no idea what such journeys were like," she wrote, "so I had set out as if I were going from Paris to Orleans." She wanted to die and clung to the tomb of another traveller who had expired on the same path.[18]

After idling away six months at her uncle's house, Tristan bitterly realized that her prospects of fortune were nil. Her dismay at Peruvian customs and standards of living was exacerbated by an earthquake and a military uprising. In April 1834, in spite of the dangers from deserters, she left for Lima in the company of an Englishman, Valentine Smith, arriving in Lima just over a week later. Lima suited her better, though the bullfights thoroughly disgusted her. "In Lima there is no poetry, only butchery," she wrote.[19] She left Peru on a ship bound for England in July 1834, but where she disembarked is unknown. She was back in Paris by January of the following year.

Mémoires et pérégrinations d'une paria incensed her uncle but was just the first of a series of controversial books, including *Promenades dans Londres* (1840), a frankly written tour of English working-class slums, brothels and factories. Her fame as a union organizer, social reformer, divorce advocate and feminist grew, as did her husband's vitriol. He took custody of their children; she had him arrested on a charge of alleged incest. He successfully fought the accusation, then published a pamphlet denouncing her immoral ways. To top it off, in 1838 he shot her. She survived, but he was thrown in jail and served seventeen years. Tristan died of fatigue and typhoid fever in 1844, during a demanding book tour for *Union ouvrière*.[20]

Ida Pfeiffer went to South America in 1846 as part of her first journey around the world. She left Hamburg in the company of Count Berchthold, whom she had met in the Holy Land and who decided to go with her as far as Brazil upon hearing of her plans during an accidental meeting. She hoped to write a book about her travels, but she humbly qualified her ambitions, saying, "My object is merely to give a plain description of what I have seen."[21] For

"For my own part I had already congratulated myself on the tragical stories I should be able to present to my readers; I beheld them shedding tears at the narration of the sufferings we had experienced, and I already appeared to myself half a martyr. Alas! I was sadly deceived. We all remained in perfectly good health; not a sailor sank exhausted . . . and the provisions were not spoilt—they were just as bad as before." —Ida Pfeiffer[22]

a writer on the lookout for material, the crossing from Europe to
South America, though rough, was disappointingly worry-free.
But the squalor and ugliness of Rio de Janeiro gave Pfeiffer a
chance to unleash her talent for description, and architecture, cul-
ture and people did not escape criticism. Illness from the
oppressive heat increased her discomfort in Rio, then an excursion
to the settlement of Petrópolis nearly came to a disastrous end
when she and Berchthold were attacked by a knife-wielding fiend
intent on murder:

> The only weapons of defence we possessed were our parasols, if I
> except a clasp knife, which I instantly drew out of my pocket and
> opened, fully determined to sell my life as dearly as possible . . . He
> caught hold of [my parasol], which, as we were struggling for it,
> broke short off, leaving only a piece of the handle in my hand. In
> the struggle, however, he dropped his knife, which rolled a few steps
> from him; I instantly made a dash, and thought I had got it, when
> he, more quick than I, thrust me away with his feet and hands, and
> once more obtained possession of it. He waved it furiously over my
> head, and dealt me two wounds, a thrust and a deep gash, both in
> the upper part of the left arm; I thought I was lost, and despair alone
> gave me the courage to use my own knife. I made a thrust at his
> breast; this he warded off, and I only succeed in wounding him
> severely in the hand. The Count sprang forward, and seized the
> fellow from behind, and thus afforded me an opportunity of raising
> myself from the ground.[23]

Berchthold sustained a deep cut to his hand, and all would have been
lost had not help arrived just at that moment. The would-be assassin
was captured by passing horsemen, and the pair continued on to
Petrópolis. The incident had a lasting effect; Berchthold's wound laid
him up, and Pfeiffer developed a fear and mistrust of strangers that,
in the end, probably aided her survival in future tight situations.

Pfeiffer left on a four-day trek to a Puri village in the Brazilian
forest. (The Puris are now extinct.) In a disarmingly natural tone,
she narrated her solitary stay in this settlement, where she enjoyed
dining on monkey and parrot and slept rough in the hut placed at
her disposal. From Rio she sailed around Cape Horn to Valparaiso
and from there went to Tahiti.

Isabel and Richard Burton lived in Brazil from 1865 to 1867, as Richard had been appointed British consul to Brazil. They were first established in Santos, south of Rio de Janeiro, then at São Paulo. This was Isabel Burton's first big adventure; she wrote proudly to her family that "they think me a wonderful person here for being so independent, as all the ladies are namby-pamby."[24] Her health, however, was fairly delicate; she became covered in boils, caught a mild case of cholera, became a temporary home to numerous chiggers, yet rode, hiked, swam, fenced and did gymnastics.

Isabel Burton.
ILN, 22 January 1887: 98.

In 1867, she and Richard made a two-month expedition to the interior. They travelled by *char-à-banc,* mule and horse; in some places the roads were so bad that they had to lighten the load as much as possible, leaving her with only essentials: "If the ladies who travel with big baskets the size of a small cottage had seen my tiny bundle and a little leather case just big enough for brush, comb, and a very small change, they would have pitied me."[25]

She sprained her leg and returned, ignominiously, carried in a hammock, leaving Richard to travel on alone. As she approached Rio by steamer, she realized what she looked like: "I hid in the ladies' cabin, for I was ashamed of the state of my clothes . . . and I was well stared at. My boots were in shreds, my only dress had about forty slits in it, my hat was in ribbons, while my face was of a reddish mahogany hue and much swollen with exposure."[26]

Richard arrived back several months late and fell severely ill; when he recovered he became determined to leave Brazil, so the Burtons sold their belongings, and in September 1868, while Richard made another expedition, Isabel went home to England, a brief pause until her travels could resume once again. Before Richard's death in 1890 and hers in 1896, she would travel to Syria, the Holy Land, Italy, India and North Africa, and live in Damascus and Trieste. Although her final years have been tarnished by her destruction of Richard's manuscripts, the tomb she had built—in the style of a Bedouin tent—for her and her husband's remains was testimony to her love of her nomadic life.

Going Home

To fly abroad from the hive, like the bee, and return laden with the sweets of travel, scenes, which haunt the eye—wild adventures, that enliven the imagination—knowledge, to enlighten and free the mind from clinging, deadening prejudices—a wider circle of sympathy with our fellow-creatures;—these are the uses of travel, for which I am convinced every one is the better and the happier.—Mary Shelley[1]

WHETHER THEIR JOURNEYS ARE FOR SIX WEEKS OR SIX YEARS, most travellers, unless they're emigrants, assume that they will eventually return home. Most of the women in this book did just that. But even if they ended their travels in relief, the cold, damp north, after a sojourn in sunny lands, was torture; Constance Gordon Cumming advised those going home to do so in the summer.[2]

But others never returned, and it wasn't always because they wanted it that way. Alexine Tinne was murdered and Isabelle Eberhardt drowned, both in the midst of their travels. Laurence Hope took her own life. Harriet Tinne and Adriana Van Capellen died of illness, a common fate of travellers to Central Africa. Lise Cristiani was carried off by cholera in the Caucasus; Lady Annie Brassey's remains were consigned to the depths of the Indian Ocean; Hester Stanhope slowly expired in her monastery at Djoûn in Lebanon; Charlotte Canning, in spite of her advantages as the vicereine of India, died in Calcutta of a fever caught while travelling from Darjeeling; Jane Digby succumbed to fever and dysentery in Damascus.

Emmeline Wortley, too, died on the road. Her death was an accident, the result of a vicious kick in the shin received from a horse in Jerusalem. Evidently, her leg never healed and became infected. The Wortleys' maid, Coe, had already died at Aleppo.[3]

Travel significantly weakened Ida Pfeiffer, who died at the age of sixty-one, probably as a result of

Marianne North, at the end of her travels. She was photographed at her house at Alderley by Mrs. Bryan Hodgson, a neighbour.
North 1892, vol. 2, frontispiece.

fatigue and fever from her 1857 journey to Mauritius and Madagascar. Marianne North began her decline after a long and uncomfortable quarantine in the Seychelles in 1884. Although she managed to make a last voyage to Chile, she had to cut it short because of her poor health; for her the magic of travel had disappeared. She died at her home in England in 1890.

Anne Blunt solved the problem of going home by having two: Crabbet, in England, and Sheykh Obeyd, at Heliopolis, near Cairo. A knowledgeable horsewoman, she imported Arabian horses and commuted between the two estates until her death in Cairo in 1917.[4]

Considering the odds stacked against pre-twentieth-century travellers, it's a miracle that so many survived to tell their tales. And thank goodness they did, for they have left us proof that women not only got out and saw the world but also made the most of what they saw, with confidence and zest. Through their private letters, diaries and books, we have a priceless record of their many accomplishments. We can see that they paved the way for us, by breaking down barriers in their own countries and in the lands they visited. Women today question neither their right nor their ability to travel, but in taking travel for granted, perhaps we all—women and men—risk losing the spirit of adventure and sense of wonder that drove these early travellers.

Notes

INTRODUCTION: *Everywhere but Home*
1 Montagu, vol. 3, 30.
2 Fay, 175.
3 [Eastlake] *Quarterly Review,* 102; Robinson, 178, attributes the authorship of this anonymous article to Lady Elizabeth Eastlake, also a traveller and writer.
4 Cincinnati *Mirror and Ladies' Parterre,* 18 August 1832, quoted in notes, Trollope 1949 (1832), 300.
5 Calderón, 182; Martineau 1848, 263; Duff Gordon, 110; Tristan, 129.
6 Bird 1875, 58.
7 Dronsart, 129.
8 Fay, 29.
9 [Eastlake] *Quarterly Review,* 101, 99.
10 Ibid., 104, 103.
11 "Not at Home," 21 June 1856: 258.
12 Bury, vol. 2, 224; Parks, Fanny, 59.
13 Gladstone, 109; Audouard, 42.
14 "Lady Travellers in Norway," 176.
15 Gushington review, *ILN,* 18 April 1863, 438.
16 Curzon, quoted in Barr, 268.

Diligences, Douaniers & Baedeker's
1 Shelley 1996 (1817), 19, 23, 29.
2 Craven, vol. 1, lxv.
3 "Railway," 231, 261–62.
4 Bates, 59.
5 Montagu, vol. 1, 310–11.
6 Fay, 48.
7 Shelley 1996 (1844), 210–11, 140, 233; Starke, 3.
8 Shelley 1996 (1844), 218; Craven, vol. 1, 83.
9 Fanshawe, 138–39; Montagu, vol. 2, 310.
10 Kinder, 46.
11 Cust, 17–18; Schreiber, 123–24; Alcott, 241–42, 250.
12 Shelley 1996 (1844), 370, 177.
13 Starke, iii.

EUROPE: *On Tour with the Fair Sex*
1 Craven, vol. 1, xv, xxiv, 44–47.
2 Ibid., xxviii, xxxviii.
3 George Parks, 29–30.
4 Trollope 1836, 134.
5 Bury, vol. 1, 264, 295; Craven, vol. 1, lxv; Montagu, vol. 2, 359.
6 Adams, 380.
7 Trollope 1836, 194.
8 Smith, 349.

9 Shelley 1996 (1844), 69.
10 Ibid., 105, 140, 253; Baedeker, *Switzerland,* 276, 322.
11 Blessington, 60–61.
12 Ibid., 106.
13 Staël, Book 1, Part 2, 6.
14 Shelley 1996 (1844), 284.
15 Blessington, 47.
16 Ibid., 153–58.
17 Byron, quoted in Smith, 353; Shelley 1996 (1844), 53.
18 Elliot review, *ILN,* 1 July 1871, 639.
19 Blessington, 99.
20 Russell, 91–92; Robinson, 20; Walker's feat made it into *ILN,* 5 August 1871, 102.
21 Istria, quoted in Cortambert, 283–84, author's translation.
22 Edwards, 65.
23 Ibid., 191–93; Edwards review, *ILN,* 30 August 1873, 206; original reference to Cook's from Edwards, xxxi.
24 Eden review, *ILN,* October 1869, 368.
25 Craven, vol. 1, 124; Londonderry, 161.
26 Fanshawe, 127–28.
27 Ibid., xvi, xviii; the number of babies mentioned by Fanshawe totals fourteen; Bates, 13, says eighteen; Robinson, 236, says seventeen.
28 Fanshawe, 173.
29 Aulnoy, lxi.
30 Ibid., v–viii.
31 Schaw, 236.
32 Ibid., 243.
33 From *Lisbon in 1821–2–3* (1824), quoted in Cust, 192.
34 Burton, 232–33; Cust, 191.
35 Elliot, 3, 78, 171.
36 Ibid., 235–36.
37 Wollstonecraft 1796, 49; Baedeker's *Guide to Norway, Sweden, and Denmark,* xvi; Wollstonecraft 1979.
38 Londonderry, 7.
39 Ibid., 34, 6, 36.
40 Dashkov, 11–16.
41 Ibid., 115.
42 Schopenhauer, 65.
43 Ibid., 25.

RUSSIA: *Realizing the Unrealizable*
1 Londonderry, 58, 55.
2 Hommaire de Hell, 56.

3   Félinska, 210, author's translation.
4   Cristiani, 385.
5   Ibid., 394–95.
6   Marsden, 12.
7   Ibid., 21.
8   Ibid., 13.
9   Ibid., 95.
10   Ibid., 139.
11   Guthrie, title page.
12   Ibid., 15.
13   Hommaire, 205.
14   Ibid., 286–87.
15   Ibid., 208.
16   Ibid., 368–69.
17   Ibid., 387–88.
18   Cortambert, 24; the Hommaires are
     sometimes referred to as the Hells, but
     Adèle called her husband Hommaire.
19   Seacole, 2.
20   Ibid., 73.
21   "Evacuation of the Crimea," *ILN,* 30
     August 1856, 216; "Our Own Vivandiere,"
     Punch, 30 May 1857, 221.
22   Serena 1882, vol. 43, 416.
23   Ibid., vol. 43, 354.
24   Serena 1882, vol. 44, 240.

THE MIDDLE EAST: *Desert Queens*
1   Pfeiffer 1852, 41.
2   The word *dragoman* comes from the
     Arabic word for interpreter, *turjuman,*
     Cowan, 93; Martineau 1848, 24–25;
     Baedeker's *Handbook to Egypt,* xxv.
3   Pfeiffer 1852, 174.
4   Montagu, vol. 1, 356: Letter to Lady Rich,
     from Adrianople, 1 April 1717.
5   Montagu, vol. 2, 10.
6   Ibid., 70.
7   Montagu, vol. 1, 394–95.
8   Craven, vol. 2, 117–18, 101.
9   Belgiojoso, vol. 9, 474, author's translation.
10   Londonderry 1958, 218–19.
11   Victoria Wortley, quoted in Cust, 271;
     Beaufort, vol. 2, 390;
12   Gattey, 142; Belgiojoso, vol. 9, 467;
     Belgiojoso 1862 (1858), 305–307.
13   Strachey, 213.
14   Kinglake, 67–68.
15   Strachey, 214; Childs, 92.
16   Childs, 134–39.
17   Ibid., 147, 156.
18   Childs, 191, 201; Meryon, vol. 1, x.
19   Fraser, 281.
20   Digby, quoted in Lovell, 161.
21   Beaufort, vol. 1, 370.
22   Burton 1875, vol. 1, 4–7.

23   Burton 1898, 367
24   Ibid., 372, 491; Martineau 1848, 491.
25   Burton 1898, 384–85.
26   Ibid., 389.
27   Ibid., 368–69.
28   Paschkoff, 170, author's translation.
29   Ibid., 173.
30   Longford, 97.
31   Blunt 1879, 48.
32   Burton 1898, 469; Blunt 1879, vol. 2, 158–59.

EGYPT: *Leave Your Crinoline in Cairo*
1   Baedeker's *Handbook to Egypt,* 28.
2   Fay, 92, 93.
3   Roberts, 143; "Epitome of News . . ."
     ILN, 30 November 1884, 343.
4   Martineau 1848, 292.
5   Ibid., 72–73.
6   Ibid., 204.
7   Beaufort, vol. 1, 36.
8   Poole review, *Blackwood's Magazine,* March
     1845: 286–97, 290–91.
9   Beaufort, vol. 1, vii.
10   Ibid., 73.
11   Ibid., 249.
12   Pfeiffer 1852, 241; Beaufort, vol. 1, 114;
     Martineau 1848, 200.
13   Poole, quoted in "Mrs. Poole's
     'Englishwoman in Egypt,' " 296.
14   Audouard, 315, author's translation.
15   Beaufort, vol. 1, 114–15.
16   Bensly, 33.
17   Victoria Wortley, quoted in Cust, 291.
18   Pfeiffer 1852, 243.
19   Nightingale, 181; Hill, 15.
20   Audouard, 390–92.
21   Duff Gordon, 115.
22   Ibid., 186–92.
23   Ibid., 355; Martineau 1848, 40.
24   Pfeiffer 1852, 259.

AFRICA: *No Place for a Lady?*
1   Beaufort, vol. 1, 49.
2   Petherick, vol. 1, 27–28.
3   Petherick, vol. 1, 174; H. J. Holland,
     quoted in Petherick, vol. 1, 175.
4   Baker 1868, 100–101.
5   Hall, 26–29.
6   Baker review, *ILN,* 16 June 1866, 594.
7   Hall, 47; Baker 1870 (1866), 7, 69–70.
8   Baker 1870 (1866), 304.
9   Ibid., 437.
10   Gladstone, 101, 104, 106.
11   Ibid., 119.
12   Baker 1870 (1866), 20.
13   Gladstone, 123–27.

14 Petherick, vol. 1, 306.
15 Gladstone, 134–37.
16 Ibid., 149–53.
17 Ibid., 156.
18 Gladstone, 164; Petherick, vol. 2, 25.
19 Gladstone, 196–97, 202, 206.
20 *Times,* 6 September 1869, 1; Gladstone, 220–21.
21 Montagu, vol. 2, 97; Fraser, 284.
22 Crisp, ms.
23 Hart, 27.
24 Eberhardt, 2.
25 Hart, 24–31.
26 Ibid., 41–46, 60–64.
27 Kobak, 56.
28 Ibid., 49, 88–89.
29 Eberhardt, 48.
30 Kobak, 132, 137.
31 Cauvet, quoted in Kobak, 130.
32 Eberhardt, quoted in Kobak, 167.
33 Eberhardt, 46, 108; Kobak, 175, 188.
34 Falconbridge, 116; Fyfe in Falconbridge, 130–32.
35 Picard, 103, 143.
36 Frank, 64; Kingsley 1899, 95.
37 Frank, 18, 21.
38 Ibid., 31,
39 Kingsley 1897, 9; Frank, 87–88, 69, 74–78.
40 Frank, 95.
41 Kingsley 1899, 31.
42 Ibid., 122.
43 Kingsley 1897, 12, 103, 165, 203, 548.
44 Kingsley 1899, x; *Nature,* from publisher's advertisement for *Travels in West Africa.*
45 Kingsley 1899, xii, 6.
46 Frank, 220–21.
47 Kingsley 1899, 310.

ARABIA TO PERSIA: *A Desire for Danger*
1 Blunt 1881, vol. 1, 102–104.
2 Blunt 1986, 95.
3 Blunt 1881, vol. 1, 187.
4 Pfeiffer c. 1851, 245.
5 Ibid., 259, 270.
6 Pfeiffer c. 1851, 299.
7 Dieulafoy 1989, 12, 19.
8 Dieulafoy 1887, 34, author's translation.
9 Bird 1891, vol. 1, 45–47, 90–92, 152.
10 Bird 1891, vol. 2, 396.
11 Ibid., 166.

Lambs in Wolves' Clothing
1 Seacole, 20.
2 Cortambert, 16–23.
3 Ibid., 38–41.

4 Bassett, 3.
5 Thurman, 84; Klumpke, xxxi. A famous holder of such a permit was painter Rosa Bonheur. The subject of French laws forbidding the wearing of men's clothes has been the subject of numerous works.
6 Burton 1898, 419–20.
7 Pfeiffer 1852, 76.
8 Beaufort, vol. 1, 127.
9 Childs, 163; Martineau 1848, 42.

INDIA: *Forgetting to Be Shocked*
1 Fay, 111.
2 Ibid., 146.
3 Premble, 14.
4 Graham, 28.
5 Premble, 5.
6 Fane, quoted in Premble, 63, 165, 53.
7 Premble, 232, 237.
8 Duff Gordon, 267.
9 Eden, vol. 2, 116; vol. 1, 189.
10 Fane, 208; Eden, vol. 2, 11.
11 Seymour, 16–17; Eden, vol. 2, 183.
12 Longford, 152.
13 Pfeiffer c. 1851, 208.
14 Gordon Cumming, 75, 526.
15 Ibid., 323.
16 In French translations of his works, his name is given as Charles–E. d'Ujfalvy.
17 Ujfalvy, 226–27.
18 Ibid., 394.
19 Blanch, 1963.

OCEANIA: *The Round-the Worlders Converge*
1 Parker, 3, 9.
2 Ibid., 95, 89–90.
3 Ibid., 107.
4 Meredith, 119.
5 Ibid., 105–106.
6 Clacy, 52, 90–91, 75, 106.
7 Hill, 281–82.
8 Pfeiffer 1856, 184, 190.
9 Cortambert, 374.
10 Pfeiffer 1856, 74, 167.
11 Ibid., 263–64.
12 Leonowens, 8.
13 Ibid., 20–21.
14 Ibid., 57–58.
15 Ibid., 282–83.
16 Bird 1875, 102.
17 Bird 1883, 306–307.
18 Ibid., 250.
19 North, vol. 2, 141.
20 Ibid., 124–25.
21 Ibid., 337.
22 Forbes, 263.

Staying Alive

1 Pfeiffer c. 1851, 247; Belgiojoso 1862 (1858), 370–71.
2 Belgiojoso 1862 (1858), 370–71, author's translation.
3 North, vol. 1, 325, 216.
4 Belgiojoso, quoted in Gattey, 177.
5 Fanny Parks, vol. 2, 45.
6 Martineau 1848, 522.

CHINA, JAPAN & TIBET: *Faith & Folly*

1 Pfeiffer c. 1851, 94.
2 Collis, 5.
3 Pfeiffer c. 1851, 100, 95.
4 Bourboulon, 319, 324.
5 Ibid., 319.
6 Dronsart, 51; Michell, 212.
7 Bird 1881 (1880), 52.
8 Ibid., 28.
9 Ibid., 42, 68–83.
10 North, vol. 2, 212.
11 Bird, 191; Barr, 270.
12 Barr, 339–40.
13 Carey, 26, 4, 167.
14 Ibid., 148–49.
15 I have been unable to pinpoint the exact location of Lusar; Kumbum is close to the city of Xining.
16 Rijnhart, 387–88.
17 Russell, 175.

NORTH AMERICA: *Trollopizing a Continent*

1 *Cariboo*, 7.
2 Jameson, vol. 1, 2.
3 Ibid., 38, 82.
4 Ibid., 64–68.
5 Jameson, vol. 3, 28, 35.
6 Ibid., 145.
7 Ibid., 153, 166–67, 316, 321.
8 Ibid., 332–33.
9 Kirk, 394.
10 Hargrave, 219.
11 Pfeiffer 1856, 456–57.
12 Trollope 1949 (1832), 96, note.
13 Bird 1856, 125; Trollope 1949 (1832), 404.
14 Trollope 1949 (1832), 14.
15 Mullen, 72–75.
16 Martineau 1838, vol. 1, 33, 34.
17 Ibid., vol. 2, 255.
18 Ibid., 91.
19 Trollope 1949 (1832), 181.

20 Martineau 1838, vol 1, 213.
21 Martineau 1838, vol. 2, 198, 239.
22 Wortley, 56.
23 Ibid., 82.
24 Martineau 1838, vol. 1, 96; Coleridge, vol. 1, 219.
25 Trollope 1949 (1832), 385.
26 Bird 1856, 233–34.
27 Pfeiffer 1856, 302; Trollope 1949 (1832), 16; Bird 1966 (1856), 148, 170.
28 Bird 1879, 223.
29 Bird 1966 (1856), 110.
30 Seymour, 30, 32, 36, 38.
31 Ibid., 66–70, 93–94, 101.
32 Ibid., 204, 214, 219–24.

CENTRAL & SOUTH AMERICA: *Not for Namby-Pambies*

1 Seacole, 40–41; Seymour, 310–11.
2 Seacole, 18.
3 Wortley, 281.
4 [Eastlake] *Quarterly Review*, 114–15.
5 Calderón, 23.
6 Ibid., 229, 130.
7 Behn, 134, 152–58.
8 Duffy, 39–41, 32, 30, 45.
9 Davis, 168, 172, 175.
10 Ibid., 146, 157, 161–67, 178.
11 Maxwell, 315–17.
12 Ibid., 322–23.
13 Ibid., 319–31.
14 Graham, 65, 69–70.
15 Ibid., 71–75, 78.
16 Tristan, 55.
17 Ibid., 82.
18 Ibid., 84, 90.
19 Ibid., 328.
20 Ibid., xxi–xxvii.
21 Pfeiffer c. 1851, 18.
22 Ibid., 11.
23 Ibid., 34.
24 Burton 1898, 250.
25 Ibid., 278–79.
26 Ibid., 340.

Going Home

1 Shelley 1996 (1844), 157.
2 Gordon Cumming, 596.
3 Cust, 300–301, 331.
4 Longford, 408.

Bibliography

BOOKS

Adams, W. H. Davenport. *Celebrated Women Travellers of the Nineteenth Century*. London: Swan Sonnenschein, 1882.

Alcott, Louisa May. *Louisa May Alcott: Her Life, Letters, and Journals*. Ed. Ednah D. Cheney. Boston: Roberts Brothers, 1891.

Audouard, Olympe d'. *Les Mystères de l'Égypte dévoilés*. 2nd ed. Paris: E. Dentu, 1866.

Aulnoy, Marie Cathèrine Jumelle de Berneville, Comtesse d'. *Travels into Spain; Being the Ingenious and Diverting Letters of the Lady. Translated . . . from Relation du Voyage d'Espagne (1691)*. Ed. R. Foulché-Delbosc. London: George Routledge & Sons, 1931.

Baedeker, Karl. *Guide to Norway, Sweden, and Denmark*. Leipzig: Karl Baedeker, 1895.

———. *Handbook to Egypt. Part I: Lower Egypt*. Leipzig: Karl Baedeker, 1895.

———. *Switzerland*. Leipzig: Karl Baedeker, 1911.

Baker, Samuel White. *The Albert N'yanza, Great Basin of the Nile, and Exploration of Nile Sources*. London: Macmillan, 1871 (1st published 1866).

———. *The Nile Tributaries of Abyssinia, and the Sword Hunters of the Hamran Arabs*. Philadelphia: J. B. Lippincott, 1868 (1st published 1867).

Barr, Pat. *A Curious Life for a Lady: The Story of Isabella Bird, Traveller Extraordinary*. Harmondsworth: Penguin, 1985 (1st published 1970).

Bassett, Marnie. *Realms and Islands: The World Voyage of Rose de Freycinet in the Corvette Uranie, 1817–1820*. London: Oxford Univ. Press, 1962.

Bates, E. S. *Touring in 1600*. London: Century, 1987 (1st published 1911).

Beaufort, Emily A. *Egyptian Sepulchres and Syrian Shrines*. 2 vols. London: Longman, Green, Longman, & Roberts, 1861.

Behn, Aphra. "Orinooko: Or, The Royal Slave." In *The Plays, Histories, and Novels of the Ingenious Mrs. Aphra Behn*. Vol. 5. London: J. Pearson, 1871 (this ed. 1st published 1735).

Belgiojoso, Cristina Trivulzia Barbiano di, Princess. *Oriental Harems and Scenery*. New York: Carleton, 1862 (1st published in French, 1858).

Bensly, Mrs. R. L. *Our Journey to Sinai: A Visit to the Convent of St. Catarina*. London: The Religious Tract Society, 1896.

Bird, Isabella Lucy. *An Englishwoman in America*. Introduction by Andrew Hill Clark. Madison, Milwaukee: Univ. of Wisconsin Press, 1966 (1st published 1856).

———. *The Golden Chersonese and the Way Thither*. London: John Murray, 1883.

———. *The Hawaiian Archipelago: Six Months among the Palm Groves, Coral Reefs and Volcanoes of the Sandwich Islands*. London: John Murray, 1875.

———. *Journeys in Persia and Kurdistan: Including a Summer in the Upper Karun Region and a Visit to the Nestorian Rayahs*. 2 vols. London: John Murray, 1891.

———. *A Lady's Life in the Rocky Mountains*. London: John Murray, 1910 (1st published 1879).

———. *Unbeaten Tracks in Japan: An Account of Travels on Horseback in the Interior Including Visits to the Aborigines of Yezo and the Shrines of Nikkó and Isé*. 2 vols. New York: G.P. Putnam, 1881 (1st published 1880).

———. *The Yangtze Valley and Beyond: An Account of Journeys in China, Chiefly in the Province of Sze Chuan and among the Mantze of the Somo Territory*. London: John Murray, 1899.

Blanch, Leslie. *Under a Lilac-Bleeding Star: Travels and Travellers*. London: John Murray, 1963.

Blessington, Marguerite, Countess of. *Lady Blessington at Naples*. Excerpts from *The Idler in Italy*. Ed. Edith Clay. London: H. Hamilton, 1979.

Blunt, Lady Anne. *Bedouin Tribes of the Euphrates*. 2 vols. London: John Murray, 1879.

———. *Journals and Correspondence, 1878–1917*. Ed. Rosemary Archer and James Fielding. Cheltenham, U.K.: Alexander Heriot, 1986.

———. *A Pilgrimage to Nejd: The Cradle of the Arab Race. A Visit to the Court of the Arab Emir, and "Our Persian Campaign."* 2 vols. London: John Murray, 1881.

Brassey, Lady Annie. *The Last Voyage, 1886–1887*. London: Longmans, Green, 1889.

Burton, Lady Isabel. *The Inner Life of Syria, Palestine, and the Holy Land*. 2 vols. London: H. S. King, 1875.

Burton, Lady Isabel, and W. H. Wilkins. *The Romance of Isabel Lady Burton: The Story of Her Life.* London: Hutchinson, 1898.

Bury, Lady Charlotte. *The Diary of a Lady-in-Waiting: Being the Diary Illustrative of the Times of George the Fourth [etc.].* 2 vols. London: John Lane, 1908.

Calderón de la Barca, Frances Erskine. *Life in Mexico: During a Residence of Two Years in that Country.* London: Chapman & Hall, 1843.

Carey, William, ed. *Adventures in Tibet: Including the Diary of Miss Annie R. Taylor's Remarkable Journey from Tay-Chau to Ta-Chien-Lu Through the Heart of the Forbidden Land.* London: Hoddert & Stoughton, 1902.

Cariboo: The Newly Discovered Gold Fields of British Columbia. Reprint: Fairfield, Washington: Ye Galleon Press, 1975 (1st published 1862).

Childs, Virginia. *Lady Hester Stanhope: Queen of the Desert.* London: Weidenfeld & Nicolson, 1990.

Clacy, Ellen (Mrs. Charles). *A Lady's Visit to the Gold Diggings of Australia, 1852–53, Written on the Spot.* Melbourne: Lansdowne Press, 1963 (1st published 1853).

Coleridge, Edith, ed. *Memoir and Letters of Sara Coleridge.* Vol. 1. London: Henry S. King, 1873.

Collis, Maurice. *Foreign Mud.* London: Faber & Faber, 1946.

Cortambert, Richard. *Les Illustres voyageuses.* Paris: Maillet, 1866.

Cowan, J. M., ed. *The Hans Wehr Dictionary of Modern Written Arabic.* Ithaca, N.Y.: Spoken Languages Services, 1976.

Craven, Lady Elizabeth. *The Beautiful Lady Craven: The Original Memoirs [etc.]. (1790–1828).* Ed. A. M. Broadley and Lewis Melville. 2 vols. London: John Lane, 1914.

Crisp, Elizabeth. *Diary of her Captivity in Barbary, in the year 1756.* Ms. Collection of the Charles E. Young Research Library, Special Collections, UCLA.

Cust, Nina. *Wanderers: Episodes from the Travels of Lady Emmeline Stuart-Wortley and Her Daughter Victoria 1849–1855.* New York: Coward-McCann, 1928.

Dashkov, Princess Catherine Vorontsov. *The Memoirs of Princess Dashkov.* Trans. and ed. Kyril Fitzlyon. London: John Calder, 1958.

Davis, Natalie Zemon. *Women on the Margins: Three Seventeenth-Century Lives.* Cambridge, Mass.: Harvard Univ. Press, 1995.

Dieulafoy, Jane. *Une Amazone en Orient.* Ed. Chantal Edel and Jean-Pierre Sicre. Paris: Phébus, 1989.

Dronsart, Marie. *Les Grandes voyageuses.* Paris: Hachette, 1894.

Duff Gordon, Lady Lucie. *Letters from Egypt: 1862–1869.* Ed. Gordon Waterfield. London: Routledge & Kegan Paul, 1969 (1st published 1865 and 1875).

Duffy, Maureen. *The Passionate Shepherdess: Aphra Behn 1640–90.* London: Jonathan Cape, 1977.

Duyckinck, Ewart A. *Portrait Gallery of Eminent Men and Women, with Biographies.* Vol. 2. New York: Johnson Wilson, 1874.

Eberhardt, Isabelle. *The Passionate Nomad: The Diary of Isabelle Eberhardt.* Trans. Nina de Voogd. Boston: Beacon Press, 1987.

Eden, Hon. Emily. *Up the Country: Letters Written to Her Sister from the Upper Provinces of India.* 2 vols. London: Richard Bentley, 1866.

Edwards, Amelia. *Untrodden Peaks and Unfrequented Valleys: A Midsummer Ramble in the Dolomites.* London: Longmans, Green, 1873.

Elliot, Frances Minto. *Diary of an Idle Woman in Spain.* 2 vols. London: F. V. White, 1884.

Falconbridge, Anna Maria. *Narrative of Two Voyages to the River Sierra Leone, During the Years 1791–2–3.* Ed. Christopher Fyfe. Liverpool: Liverpool Univ. Press, 2000 (1st published 1794).

Fanshawe, Lady Ann. *The Memoirs of Anne, Lady Halkett and Ann, Lady Fanshawe.* Ed. John Loftis. Oxford: Clarendon Press, 1979.

Fay, Mrs. Eliza. *Original Letters from India: Containing a Narrative of a Journey Through Egypt, and the Author's Imprisonment at Calicut by Hyder Ally: 1779–1815.* Introduction by E. M. Forster. London: Hogarth Press, 1925 (1st published 1817).

Forbes, Anna. *Unbeaten Tracks in Islands of the Far East: Experiences of a Naturalist's Wife in the 1880s.* Singapore: Oxford Univ. Press, 1987 (1st published as *Insulinde,* 1887).

Fountaine, Margaret. *Love Among the Butterflies: The Secret Life of a Victorian Lady.* Ed. W. F. Cater. Boston: Little, Brown, 1980.

Frank, Katherine. *A Voyager Out: The Life of Mary Kingsley.* New York: Ballentine, 1986.

Fraser, Flora. *The Unruly Queen: The Life of Queen Caroline.* New York: Alfred A. Knopf, 1996.

Gattey, Charles Nielson. *A Bird of Curious Plumage: The Life of Princess Cristina di*

Belgiojoso, 1808–1871. London: Constable, 1971.

Gladstone, Penelope. *Travels of Alexine: Alexine Tinne, 1835–1869*. London: John Murray, 1970.

Gordon Cumming, Constance F. *In the Himalayas and on the Indian Plains*. 2 vols. New York: Scribner's, 1884.

Graham, Maria Dundas. *The Captain's Wife: The South American Journals of Maria Graham, 1821–23*. Ed. Elizabeth Mavor. London: Weidenfeld & Nicolson, 1993.

———. *Journal of a Residence in India*. Edinburgh: Archibald Constable, et al., 1812.

Guthrie, Mrs. Maria. *A Tour, Performed in the Years 1795–6, Through the Taurida, or Crimea, The Antient Kingdom of Bosphorus . . . Described in a Series of Letters to Her Husband, the Editor, etc.* London: T. Cadell, 1802.

Hall, Richard. *Lovers on the Nile: The Incredible African Journeys of Sam and Florence Baker*. New York: Random House, 1980.

Hardy, Lady Mary Duffus. *Through Cities and Prairie Lands: Sketches of an American Tour*. New York: R. Worthington, 1881.

Hargrave, Letitia. *The Letters of Letitia Hargrave*. Ed. Margaret Arnett Macleod. Toronto: The Champlain Society, 1947.

Hart, Ursula Kingsmill. *Two Ladies of Colonial Algeria: The Lives and Time of Aurélie Picard and Isabelle Eberhardt*. Athens, Ohio: Ohio Univ. Center for International Studies, Monographs in International Studies, African Series No. 49, 1987.

Hill, Florence, and Rosamond Hill. *What We Saw in Australia*. London: Macmillan, 1875.

[Hommaire de Hell, Adèle], and Xavier Hommaire de Hell. *Travels in the Steppes of the Caspian Sea, The Crimea, The Caucasus, &c.* London: Chapman & Hall, 1847.

Jameson, Anna. *Winter Studies and Summer Rambles in Canada*. Toronto: McClelland & Stewart, 1923 (1st published 1838).

Kinder, Hermann, and Werner Hilgemann. *The Penguin Atlas of World History*. Vol. 2. Trans. Ernest A. Menze. Harmondsworth: Penguin, 1978.

Kinglake, A. W. *Eothen*. London: Century, 1982 (1st published 1844).

Kingsley, Mary Henrietta. *Travels in West Africa*. London: Macmillan, 1897.

———. *West African Studies*. London: Macmillan, 1899.

Kirk, Sylvia Van. "Gunn, Isabel" in *Dictionary of Canadian Biography*. Vol. 5, 1801 to 1820. Toronto: Univ. of Toronto Press, 1983.

Klumpke, Anna. *Rosa Bonheur: The Artist's (Auto)biography*. Trans. Gretchen van Slyke. Ann Arbor: Univ. of Michigan Press, 1997.

Kobak, Annette. *Isabelle: The Life of Isabelle Eberhardt*. New York: Vintage Books, 1990.

Leonowens, Anna H. *The English Governess at the Siamese Court*. Boston: J. R. Osgood, 1871.

Londonderry, Edith, Marchioness of. *Frances Anne: The Life and Times of Frances Anne Marchioness of Londonderry and her husband Charles Third Marquess of Londonderry*. London: Macmillan, 1958.

Londonderry, Frances Anne, Marchioness of. *Russian Journal of Lady Londonderry, 1836–37*. Ed. W. A. L. Seaman & J. R. Sewell. London: John Murray, 1973.

Longford, Elizabeth. *A Pilgrimage of Passion: The Life of Wilfrid Scawen Blunt*. London: Weidenfeld & Nicolson, 1979.

Lovell, Mary S. *Rebel Heart: The Scandalous Life of Jane Digby*. New York: W. W. Norton, 1995.

Marsden, Kate. *On Sledge and Horseback to Outcast Siberian Lepers*. London: Record Press, 1893.

Martineau, Harriet. *Eastern Life, Present and Past*. Philadelphia: Lea & Blanchard, 1848.

———. *Retrospect of Western Travel*. 3 vols. London: Saunders & Otley, 1838.

Maxwell, Patrick, ed. "Voyage of Madame Godin along the River of the Amazons, in the Year 1770." In *Perils and Captivity [etc.]*. Edinburgh: Constable, 1827.

Meredith, Louisa Anne. *Notes and Sketches of New South Wales: During a Residence in that Colony from 1839 to 1844*. London: John Murray, 1844.

[Meryon, Charles L.] *Memoirs of the Lady Hester Stanhope: As Related by Herself in Conversations with Her Physician; Comprising Her Opinions and Anecdotes of Some of the Most Remarkable Persons of Her Time*. 3 vols. London: H. Colburn, 1846.

Michell, T. *Handbook for Travellers to Russia, Poland, and Finland*. London: John Murray, 1865.

Middleton, Dorothy. *Victorian Lady Travellers*. Chicago: Academy, 1965.

Montagu, Lady Mary Wortley. *The Letters and Works of Lady Mary Wortley Montagu*. 3 vols. Ed. Lord Wharncliffe. London: Richard Bentley, 1837.

Mullen, Richard. *Birds of Passage: Five Englishwomen in Search of America*. New York: St. Martin's Press, 1994.

Nightingale, Florence. *Letters from Egypt: A*

Journey on the Nile, 1849–1850. Ed. Anthony Sattin. New York: Weidenfeld & Nicolson, 1987.

Noble, Anne. *Narrative of the Shipwreck of the "Kite" and of the Imprisonment and Sufferings of the Crew and Passengers; in a Letter from Mrs. Anne Noble to a Friend.* Macao: Canton Press, 1841.

North, Marianne. *Recollections of a Happy Life.* Ed. Mrs. J. A. Symonds. 2 vols. London: Macmillan, 1892.

——. *Some Further Recollections of a Happy Life.* Ed. Mrs. J. A. Symonds. London: Macmillan, 1893.

Parker, Mary Ann. *A Voyage Round the World.* Ed. Gavin Fry. Sydney: Horden House & Australian National Maritime Museum, 1991 (1st published 1795).

Parks, Fanny. *Wanderings of a Pilgrim in Search of the Picturesque.* 2 vols. Karachi: Oxford Univ. Press, 1975 (1st published 1850).

Parks, George B. *The English Traveler to Italy.* Vol. 1: The Middle Ages (to 1525). Stanford, CA: Stanford Univ. Press, 1954.

Petherick, John, and Katherine Harriet Petherick. *Travels in Central Africa and Explorations of the Western Nile Tributaries.* London: Tinsley, 1869.

Pfeiffer, Ida. *A Lady's Second Journey Round the World.* New York: Harper & Brothers, 1856.

——. *Visit to the Holy Land, Egypt, and Italy.* London: Ingram, Cooke, 1852.

——. *A Woman's Journey Round the World, from Vienna to Brazil, Chili, Tahiti, China, Hindostan, Persia, and Asia Minor.* London: Office of the Nat. Illustrated Library, [1851].

[Picard] Dard, C. A. "The Suffering and Misfortunes of the Picard Family, After the Shipwreck of the *Medusa,* on the Western Coast of Africa, in the Year 1816." In *Perils and Captivity [etc.].* Ed. Patrick Maxwell. Edinburgh: Constable, 1827.

Premble, John, ed. *Miss Fane in India.* Gloucester: Alan Sutton, 1985.

"Railway," in *The Encyclopaedia Britannica.* Vol. 20. Philadelphia: J. M. Stoddart, 1886.

Rijnhart, Susie Carson. *With the Tibetans in Tent and Temple: Narrative of Four Years' Residence on the Tibetan Border, and of a Journey into the Far Interior.* New York: Fleming, H. Revell, 1901.

Roberts, Emma. *Notes of an Overland Journey through France and Egypt to Bombay.* London: W. H. Allen, 1841.

Robinson, Jane. *Wayward Women: A Guide to Women Travellers.* Oxford: Oxford Univ.

Press, 1990.

Russell, Mary. *The Blessings of a Good Thick Skirt: Women Travellers and Their World.* London: Collins, 1988.

Schaw, Janet. *Journal of a Lady of Quality.* Ed. Evangeline W. Andrews and Charles McL. Andrews. 3rd ed. New Haven: Yale Univ. Press, 1939 (1st published 1921).

Schopenhauer, Johanna. *A Lady Travels: Journeys in England and Scotland from the Diaries of Johanna Schopenhauer.* Trans. and ed. Ruth Michaelis-Jena and Willy Merson. London: Routledge, 1988.

Schreiber, Lady Charlotte. *Lady Charlotte Schreiber's Journals: Confidences of a Collector of Ceramics and Antiques Throughout Britain, France, Holland, Belgium, Spain, Portugal, Turkey, Austria, and Germany From the Years 1869 to 1885.* Ed. Montague J. Guest [etc.]. 2 vols. London: John Lane, 1911.

Seacole, Mrs. Mary. *Wonderful Adventures of Mrs. Seacole in Many Lands.* Ed. W. J. S. Introduction by W. J. Russell, Esq. New York: Oxford Univ. Press, 1988 (1st published 1857).

Serena, Carla. *De la Baltique à la Caspienne. Souvenirs personnels.* Paris: Dreyfous, 1881.

Seymour, Bruce. *Lola Montez: A Life.* New Haven: Yale Univ. Press, 1996.

Shelley, Mary. *History of a Six Weeks' Tour, Letters from Geneva I and II,* and *Rambles in Germany and Italy. The Novels and Selected Works of Mary Shelley. Vol. 8, Travel Writing.* Ed. Jeanne Moskal. London: William Pickering, 1996 (1st published 1817 and 1844).

Sillitoe, Alan. *Leading the Blind: A Century of Guide Book Travel, 1815–1914.* London: Macmillan, 1995.

Smith, George Barnett. *Women of Renown.* New York: Books for Libraries Press, 1972 (1st published 1893).

Staël, Anne-Louise-Germaine, de. *Corinne, or Italy.* Trans. Avriel H. Goldgerger. New Brunswick, N.J.: Rutgers Univ. Press, 1987 (1st published 1807).

Starke, Mariana. *Travels in Europe, for the Use of Travellers on the Continent, and Likewise in the Island of Sicily [etc.].* 9th ed. Paris: A. & W. Galignani, 1839 (1st published 1820).

Strachey, Lytton. "Lady Hester Stanhope." In *Biographical Essays.* London: Chatto & Windus, 1960.

Thurman, Judith. *Secrets of the Flesh: A Life of Colette.* New York: Alfred A. Knopf, 1999.

Tristan, Flora. *Peregrinations of a Pariah.* Trans. and ed. Jean Hawkes. Boston: Beacon Travellers, 1987 (1st published 1838).

Trollope, Frances Milton. *Domestic Manners of the Americans*. Ed. Donald Smalley. New York: Alfred A. Knopf, 1949 (1st published 1832).

———. *Paris and the Parisians in 1835*. New York: Harper & Brothers, 1836.

Tully, (Miss). *Narrative of a Ten Years' Residence at Tripoli in Africa: From the Original Correspondence in the Possession of the Family of the Late Richard Tully, Esq., the British Consul*. London: H. Colburn, 1816.

Withey, Lynne. *Grand Tours and Cook's Tours: A History of Leisure Travel: 1750 to 1915*. New York: William Morrow, 1997.

Wollstonecraft, Mary. *Collected Letters of Mary Wollstonecraft*. Ed. Ralph M. Wardle. Ithaca: Cornell Univ. Press, 1979.

———. *Letters Written during a Short Residence in Sweden, Norway, and Denmark*. London: J. Johnson, 1796.

Wortley, Lady Emmeline Charlotte Elizabeth (Manners) Stuart. *Travels in the United States, etc. During 1849 and 1850*. New York: Harper & Brothers, 1851.

PERIODICALS

ILN = *Illustrated London News*

Belgiojoso, Cristina Trivulzia Barbiano di, Princess. "La Vie intime et la vie nomade en Orient, scènes et souvenirs de voyage." In *Revue des deux mondes* 9, 1 février 1855: 466–501.

Bourboulon, Catherine de, and Achille Poussielgue. "Relation de voyage de Shang-Haï à Moscou, par Pekin, la Mongolie et la Russie Asiatique, rédigée d'après les notes de M de Bourboulon, Ministre de France en Chine, et de Mme de Bourboulon, 1860–1862." In *Tour du monde* 10, 1864: 289–336; 11, 1865: 233–72.

Cristiani, Lise. "Voyage dans la Sibérie orientale." In *Tour du monde* 7, 1863: 385–400.

Dieulafoy, Jane. "La Perse, la Chaldée et la Susiane, 1881–1882." In *Tour du monde* 46, 1883: 81–160.

———. "A Suse, journal des fouilles 1884–1886." In *Tour du monde* 54, 1887: 1–96; 55, 1887: 1–80; 56, 1887: 81–160.

[Eastlake, Lady Elizabeth] "Lady Travellers." In *Quarterly Review* 151, 1845: 98–137.

"Epitome of News—Foreign and Domestic." In *ILN*, 30 November 1844: 343.

"Evacuation of the Crimea." In *ILN*, 30 August 1856: 216.

Félinska, Ève. "De Kiew à Bérézov, souvenir d'une exilée en Sibérie (1839)." In *Tour du monde* 6, 1862: 209–40.

"Lady Travelers in Norway." In *Eclectic Magazine*, 1858: 176–87.

"Murder of Mdlle. Tinne in the Interior of Africa." In the London *Times*, 6 September 1869: 10.

"Not at Home." In *Punch*, 21 June 1856: 258.

"Our Own Vivandiere." In *Punch*, 30 May 1857: 221.

Paschkoff, Lydie. "Voyage à Palmyre (1872)." In *Tour du monde* 33, 1872: 161–76.

Serena, Carla. "Excursion au Samourzakan et en Abkasie (1881)." In *Tour du monde* 43, 1882: 353–416.

———. "Trois mois en Kakhétie (1877–81)." In *Tour du monde* 44, 1882: 193–208, 225–40.

Ujfalvy-Bourdon, Marie de. "Voyage d'une parisienne dans l'Himalaya occidental: le Koulou, le Cachemire, le Baltistan et le Dras (1881)." In *Tour du monde* 46, 1883: 353–416.

BOOK REVIEWS
The following book reviews were anonymous.

Baker, Samuel White. *The Albert N'yanza, Great Basin of the Nile, and Exploration of Nile Sources*. London: Macmillan, 1866. Reviewed in *ILN*, 16 June 1866: 594.

Eden, Lizzie Selina. *My Holiday in Austria*. London: Hurst & Blackett, 1869. Reviewed in *ILN*, October 1869: 368.

Edwards, Amelia. *Untrodden Peaks and Unfrequented Valleys: A Midsummer Ramble in the Dolomites*. London: Longmans, Green, 1873. Reviewed in *ILN*, 30 August 1873: 206.

Elliot, Frances Minto. *Diary of an Idle Woman in Italy*. 2 vols. London: Chapman & Hall, 1871. Reviewed in *ILN*, 1 July 1871: 639.

Gushington, Impulsia, Hon. *Lispings from Low Latitudes; or, Extracts from the Journal of the Honourable Impulsia Gushington*. Ed. Lord Dufferin. London: John Murray, 1863. Reviewed in *ILN*, 18 April 1863: 438.

"Mrs. Poole's 'Englishwoman in Egypt.'" Review of *The Englishwoman in Egypt: Letters from Cairo . . .*, by Sophie Lane Poole. *Blackwood's Magazine*, March 1845: 286–97.

Acknowledgements

I AM INDEBTED TO THE STAFF of the University of British Columbia Main Library, and especially to Bonita Stableford, Wayne Mackay and Felicity Nagai for enthusiastically helping me with my research. A special thanks, too, to Victoria Steele, Head, Department of Special Collections and Anne Caiger, Manuscripts Curator, at the Charles E. Young Research Library, UCLA, for unearthing the Eliza Crisp manuscript, as well as other remarkable documents; and to Romaine Ahlstrom, Head of Reader Services, The Huntington Library, for showing me some of the treasures from the Huntington's remarkable collection. Thanks to everyone who suggested travellers; I wish I could have included them all, and to Saeko Usukawa, who tracked down Frances Anne Hopkins sources; to my editor, Nancy Flight, who patiently sorted through the inundation of material; to copy editor Maureen Nicholson, who did a remarkable job of coping with all the dates, names and myriad other details; and to David Gay, as ever.

CHAPTER OPENING IMAGES: *pages 1, 13, 55, 73, 137, 201:* Our Journey Around the World with Glimpses of Life in Far Off Lands as Seen Through a Woman's Eyes *by Rev. Francis E. Clark and Harriet E. Clark, Hartford, Conn.: A.D. Worthington, 1894; page 21: drawing of the Lion's Court, Alhambra, by David Roberts, engraving by Freebairn,* Jennings Landscape Annual for 1835, or The Tourist in Spain *by Thomas Roscoe, London: Robert Jennings, 1835; page 109:* The Art of Travel *by Francis Galton, London: John Murray, 1860, 56; page 123: a* Bareilly dandy, *from* The Indian Alps and How We Crossed Them *by Nina Mazuchelli, London: Longmans, Green, 1876; page 153: "Tabloid" medical kit from Burroughs Wellcome and Co, advertised in* Hints to Travellers *by E. A. Reeves, London: The Royal Geographical Society, 1906; page 157: Lady Brassey in Japan, ILN, 22 October 1887: 483; page 169: "The Conductor,"* United States Pictures *by Richard Lovett, London: The Religious Tract Society, 1891, 135; page 187: Travelling Brazilian Woman, The* Iconographic Encyclopaedia of Science, Literature and Art *by J. G. Heck, New York: Rudolph Garrigue, 1851.*

Index